Revolutionary Portraits

John Coltrane
JAZZ, RACISM AND RESISTANCE

Martin Smith

John Coltrane – jazz, racism and resistance

by Martin Smith

First published in 2001 as a Redwords Revolutionary Portrait

Extended version first published 2003 by Redwords

Reprinted with corrections 2006 by

REDWORDS

1 Bloomsbury Street, London WC1B 3QE

www.redwords.org.uk

© Martin Smith 2003

ISBN: 1 872208 22 3

Design and production: Roger Huddle, Farah Reza and Hannah Dee

Printed by Cambridge Printing, Cambridge

Redwords is linked to Bookmarks, the socialist bookshop

www.bookmarks.uk.com

Coltrane listening

contents

Acknowledgements

Many thanks to Charlie Hore, Roger Huddle, Emma Bircham and John Rees for all their valuable advice and suggestions. I would also like to thank Judith Orr for her constant support, and for being a trusted sounding board for all my ideas.

This book is dedicated to my nan and grandad, Ivy and Tom Horner, and to all those fighting racism and exploitation, wherever they may be.

Introduction

> When a black musician picks up his horn and starts
> blowing, he improvises, he creates, it comes from
> within. It's his soul. Jazz is the only area in America
> where the black man is free to create.[1]

That was how Malcolm X described the spirit of jazz at a
political rally he held in New York in 1964. Sitting in the audience was the jazz musician John Coltrane. Many of the hopes
and aspirations Malcolm eloquently expressed in his speeches
were echoed in Coltrane's music. In the words of writer Craig
Werner, 'They shared a determination that could be boiled
down to a clear central message – "Change the world now".'[2]

Coltrane started his jazz career playing the tenor saxophone, but then went on to develop and popularise the smaller
(and, until then, rarely played) soprano saxophone. Coltrane

was an ever-restless experimenter, always searching for new sounds, always pushing back the boundaries of jazz. In an era dominated by mass production, war and poverty, Coltrane's music offered hope, love and a yearning for freedom.

There have been several books written about Coltrane, so why write another one? All the previous studies have concentrated solely on the biographical details of his life. The one exception is *John Coltrane and the Jazz Revolution of the 1960s* by Frank Kofsky, which concentrates on a short period of Coltrane's musical career. I want to look at the broader picture of how jazz and the music of Coltrane were shaped by the rapidly changing world and the unique political period in which he grew up.

The Russian revolutionary Leon Trotsky argued in his book *Literature and Revolution*, 'Art should in the first place be judged by its own laws, that is, by the law of art. But Marxism alone can explain why and how a given tendency in art has originated in a given period of history'.[3]

Music critic and author LeRoi Jones (Amiri Baraka) extends the argument even further. He states in his wonderful book *Blues People*, 'The most expressive black music of any given period will portray the Negro at that particular time'.[4] For example, who would deny that 'Negro' spirituals arose from black people resisting slavery, or that rap music today highlights the brutality of life in the black ghettos of the US? I want to argue that the origins and development of jazz music can only be explained by looking at the impact racism has had on the life of black Americans. Despite facing discrimination in every aspect of their lives, black Americans have created some of the most innovative, exciting and complex music ever. The great jazz composer and bandleader Duke Ellington put it far better than I ever could, when in 1931 he wrote:

> My men and my race are the inspiration of my work. I try to catch the character and mood and feeling of my people. The music of my race is something more than the American idiom. It is the result of our transplantation to American soil and was our reaction in plantation days to the life we lived. What we could not say openly we expressed in music. The characteristic melancholic music of my race has been forged from the very white heat of our sorrows and from our gropings. I think the music of my race is something that is going to live, something which posterity will honour in a higher sense than merely that of music of the ballroom.[5]

In some ways Ellington's dream has come true – jazz is no longer treated as just entertainment. It is fast becoming America's 'classical music'. Yet for much of the 20th century jazz was both at the cutting edge of musical development and associated with the political struggles of the times. It is of course true that most jazz musicians do not write and perform music to change the world. However, as McCoy Tyner, the pianist in John Coltrane's band, recently said, 'Because society thinks that black people are inferior, any black person who produces something beautiful and artistic automatically challenges those prejudices. Therefore by definition jazz is opposed to all forms of racism and oppression'.[6]

There has always been a tradition in jazz of conscious rebellion and resistance to the indignities of racism. Duke Ellington was a standard bearer for black pride, and on many occasions played benefits for organisations linked to the US Communist Party. In 1931 trumpet player Louis Armstrong was arrested for refusing to give up his seat to a white person on a bus in Memphis.[7] Twenty five years later, when Martin Luther King was leading the civil rights movement, many in the jazz community rallied to his support. Then, when the Black Power movement swept across the US in the late 1960s, it was John Coltrane's driving music with which many of those revolutionaries identified.

This small book is an attempt both to capture the dynamism and excitement of those times, and to celebrate the courage and creativity of John Coltrane and all the other jazz pioneers.

*Over 200,000 gather near the Washington Memorial, August 1963. It was here that Martin Luther King made his 'I have a dream' speech. Overleaf: John Coltrane from the cover of **A Love Supreme**, photograph by Bob Theile.*

01 / The early years

At the stroke of midnight on 16 January 1920 America went dry. For the next 13 years it was illegal to buy or sell alcohol. But rather than discourage drinking and partying, prohibition, as it was called, had the opposite effect. Thousands of illegal drinking dens and nightclubs opened – the 'roaring 20s' had begun. The novelist F Scott Fitzgerald called the 1920s 'the most expensive orgy in history'. This explosion of hedonism was a desperate attempt to escape the horrors of the First World War, and an expression of the confidence of the middle class as the US economy expanded. There was a belief that the good times were never going to end.

This economic growth was accompanied by a transformation of the lives of a vast number of people. The inventions of the 1890s and 1900s, which had previously been restricted to a handful of rich people, were now available for mass use – the electric light, cinema and telephone. These new inventions not only improved people's lives – they brought about massive changes in art and music. There had always been popular music, but with the exception of religious and classical music, it was restricted to regions or local areas. The reason for this was simple – the vast majority of the world's population lived in isolation from one another. The development of cities in the 18th and 19th centuries had begun to change all that. Out of this industrial expansion came dance halls, sheet music and clubs, and with the mass production of the radio and gramophone player, music and culture were opened up to a worldwide audience.

Despite the improvements in the economy during the first half of the 1920s, life for the vast majority of black and white people was hard. Blues singer Bessie Smith sang in 1927:

Mister rich man, rich man,
Open up your heart and mind
Mister rich man, rich man,
Open up your heart and mind
Give the poor man a chance,
Help stop these hard, hard times.
Please listen to my pleadin',
Cause I can't stand these hard times long,
Aw listen to my pleadin',
Cause I can't stand these hard times long,
They'll make an honest man
Do things that you know is wrong.

Jazz developed around the turn of the century – but the music it derives from is much older. The roots of jazz can be traced back to Africa. However, the music also contains elements of European hymns, French folk songs, Spanish dances and black gospel music. All these music forms influenced jazz, but it was not a continuation of these musical traditions. Instead it moved off on its own musical path of development.

At the turn of the 20th century most blacks in the US lived in rural areas in the South. But that all changed with the onset of the First World War. To fight the war the army was forced to recruit large numbers of black people. Over 360,000 blacks entered military service in the five years after 1917. These soldiers fought in segregated units.

The war also put a massive strain on the US economy. To keep up with demand, industries were forced to undergo massive levels of expansion. Racist employment practices meant that before the First World War blacks were kept out of most factory jobs. But the war meant there was a shortage of workers. Industrialists and government bodies opened up jobs in the expanding war industries to black people and women. Around 750,000 blacks migrated from the rural South to the North to find work. The combined black populations of New York, Chicago, Philadelphia and Detroit almost doubled between 1910 and 1919.[1]

The growing black working class had money to spend and leisure time in which to do it. They wanted to be entertained. Jazz music filled the vacuum – it became the popular music of the 1920s and 1930s. It expressed the daring and excitement of the times. Jazz was urban music centred on New Orleans,

New York and Kansas City, not the Mississippi Delta or the Alabama cotton fields. It is the music of black urban America. To many these seemed the years of hope. Writing, painting, poetry and music all flourished in the black ghettos of the Northern cities – these were the years of the 'Harlem Renaissance'.

A central component of jazz music was and still is the blues. However, this was not the blues of the South, where blacks were tied down to the land, surrounded by innumerable restrictions. The blues in jazz expressed life in the ghettos – the hopes, disappointments, sexual adventure and growing political confidence of the age. Trumpeter Dizzy Gillespie put it this way: 'The blues of jazz is not the blues of a man raised in the social conditions of Jim Crow, poverty and squalor. It is the blues of the black working people'.[2]

John Coltrane was born on 23 September 1926 in Hamlet, North Carolina. Shortly afterwards he and his family moved to the larger town of High Point. His father was a tailor and his mother, Alice, was a seamstress and a domestic servant. Alice had attended college, and sang and played piano. His father also played various stringed instruments. Both parents were the children of Methodist ministers. Besides the parlour music his parents would play, the sounds the young Coltrane grew up with were the hymns and music of the church, the country blues of the street musicians and the swing bands he heard on the radio. The great trumpeter Don Cherry described the influence of music on black families: 'If you're born into a black family you're born into music. You're around dancing and singing all the time, you shoot craps to music, you shoot marbles to music, then when you go to church it's music all the time.'

But it was the combination of religion (spirituality) and politics that would play an important role in Coltrane's musical sound in later years:

> Both my grandfathers were ministers. I was going to church every Sunday and stuff like that, being under the influence of my grandfather – he was the dominating cat in the family. He was well versed, active politically. My father never seemed to say too much. He just went about his business and that was it. But my grandfather was pretty militant, you know. Politically inclined and everything.[3]

The grandfather in question was the Reverend William Blair. He was more of a community leader than a pulpit-pounder. In fact he was a supporter of the black nationalist Marcus Garvey. Garvey organised the 'back to Africa movement' and also advocated the setting up of black owned businesses and community organisations. Coltrane's cousin Mary Lyerly – for whom he would compose the tune 'Cousin Mary' – said:

> Our grandfather was instrumental in opening one of the first black schools in High Point where we were raised – the elemementary school that we attended. He always fought for us. Christmas time we always got books...we had Langston Hughes, Paul Laurence Dunbar, [all] sorts of black books.[4]

Six months after Coltrane was born and hundreds of miles away in New York, Duke Ellington was taking jazz to new and exciting levels. His band played at the famous Cotton Club in Harlem. The band's residency would last until 1931. The Cotton Club had a radio wire that transmitted broadcasts from coast to coast. Ellington's early compositions contained catchy lyrics and exotic musical scores. Nearly all of his considerable earnings were ploughed back into hiring the best jazz musicians of the era. Paul Gonsalves, James Blanton and Ben Webster were to make the Ellington band the best in the world. However, deep-seated racism meant that the nightclubs of the 1920s were segregated – the Cotton Club was open to white patrons only!

Historian Eric Hobsbawm estimates that by 1929 there were some 60,000 jazz bands and almost 200,000 professional musicians in the US.[5] The young took to jazz like later generations took to rock and roll. By 1930 every city outside the Deep South with a black population of over 60,000 had produced an important jazz band.[6] These jazz musicians were professionals. The entertainment industry, along with sport, was one of the few career avenues open to blacks.

On 29 October 1929 the bottom fell out of US capitalism – that was the day the stock market crashed, ushering in the Great Depression. Seven million US workers were made unemployed, and the wages of those in work fell by 39 percent. The Depression was also a disaster for jazz – between 1927 and 1934 record sales fell by a staggering 94 percent.[7]

Ellington's fame allowed his band to ride out the Depression. Musicians like Coleman Hawkins and Sydney

Bechet moved to Europe, where jazz was held in higher esteem. More importantly, it was where they could escape racism. Rex Stewart, a musician in Ellington's band, described his first European tour as 'the first time in my life I had the feeling of being accepted as an artist, a gentleman and a member of the human race'.[8] With the onset of the Great Depression any hope of real change for black Americans had faded. They faced massive discrimination in jobs, housing and education. In the Southern states a series of laws were in existence known as 'Jim Crow', which denied blacks the right to vote and to equal treatment. This was backed up by racist organisations like the Ku Klux Klan that burned and lynched blacks. It was like apartheid South Africa.

Even relatively well off black jazz musicians could not escape the indignities of racism. Trumpet player Roy Eldrige, who played in the Artie Shaw Band, described the traumatic experiences he encountered while touring. Once, when refused admission to a dance hall where his name was up in lights, he broke down:

When I finally did get in, I played that first set, trying to keep from crying. By the time I got through my set, the tears were rolling down my cheeks... I went up to my dressing room crying and saying to myself, why the hell did I come out here again when I knew what would happen? Man, when you're on stage you're great, but as soon as you come off, you're nothing. It's not worth the glory, not worth the money, not worth anything.[9]

By the time the young Coltrane had entered high school he too was familiar with the racism of American society. He grew up in a segregated town – his tatty school clothes and school books were hand me downs from the better funded schools for white children.

His cousin Mary notes, 'Those things John didn't like at all, they just got to him'.[10] It is clear from the interviews given by Coltrane and members of his family that he hated the so called 'separate but equal' indignities of the small-town South. In fact after reaching adulthood he would never return to High Point.

As the 1930s progressed the US economy picked up. Record sales also rose, from 10 million in 1931 to 260 million by 1941.[11] From the mid-1930s to 1946 'hot' jazz, or swing as it is better known today, was the dominant musical style. Chronologically, swing more or less coincided with the era of US president Franklin Roosevelt. Big bands playing brash, exciting music set the dance halls ablaze. Band leaders like Count Basie, Benny Goodman and Glen Miller became household names. Swing had a massive influence on US culture for 20 years, and was popular among both black and white audiences.

During the 1930s swing bands recorded over 85 percent of all records sold. Record sales rose largely thanks to the new vogue for jukeboxes, which in 1940 accounted for nearly half of all records sold.[12] In the 1920s only a small number of homes in the US had a radio, but by the end of the Depression nearly every home had one.

Coltrane's family had a radio but, as John later recalled,

'growing up in North Carolina, it was hard to get to hear jazz music – let alone hear blacks playing jazz. But every now and then the odd Ellington or Armstrong song sneaked through'.[13] At high school the young Coltrane learned to play the clarinet and later the saxophone. The first song he ever learned was the Artie Shaw arrangement of 'A Dream of Two Blue Orchids'.[14] By the age of 13 his father, grandfather Reverend William Blair and his uncle had all died. His friends at the time claim that this tragic loss meant that Coltrane became more and more introverted and he withdrew into his music. By 1939 Coltrane was playing clarinet in the school band. It was here that he learnt to play simple marching tunes and the latest swing hits.

Although black bandleaders developed swing music, it quickly attracted a host of white imitators. Some, like Benny Goodman, were genuinely excited by the music. But the fact remains that the vast majority of white bandleaders never gave credit to the originators of the music. Racism meant that white bandleader Benny Goodman was named 'King of Swing' and not Count Basie. This wasn't the first or the last time that a black music form had been taken over and 'sanitised' by whites.

The economic depression and the rise of fascism in Europe created a radicalisation in US politics. As the decade wore on there was a growth in trade union membership, and huge struggles to improve working people's conditions. The fledgling Congress of Industrial Organisations (CIO) led these struggles. There were also massive campaigns against fascism and racism. Throughout the first half of the 20th century, one political organisation played a pivotal role in all of these struggles and protest movements – the American Communist Party (CPUSA). The CPUSA was a mass of contradictions. On the one hand, it was loyal to the Soviet regime, following every twist and turn of Stalin's foreign policy, even though Stalin and his secret police had crushed the ideals of those who created the Russian Revolution. (The leaders of the revolution were either dead or, as in the case of Leon Trotsky, living in exile abroad and later murdered by one of Stalin's agents.) On the other hand, the CPUSA drew into its ranks the most class-conscious workers.

The CPUSA was a tireless champion against racism. It led the fight against racial segregation in the South over 25 years before Martin Luther King led the civil rights movement. The organisation won massive respect organising the Scottsboro Defence Campaign. Its principled stand against racism meant that a large number of black workers joined the organisation. By 1938 the CPUSA had over 1,000 black members in Harlem.[15]

It is important to note that there is no crude relationship between class struggle and music. However, only a fool would argue that music exists in a vacuum. Sometimes music can reflect ideas as they develop and at other times it responds to events. It can even give a voice to these movements.

Many musicians and artists in the 1930s became radicalised by the events of the times. There was a huge growth in left wing theatre, music and art. Although many jazz players held strong left wing political views, they tended to keep these to themselves. They regarded themselves as entertainers and avoided making overtly political statements in public or in their music. Just being a confident black man was enough to get you lynched in some states in the US (Louis Wright, a member of W C Handy's band, was lynched by Southern white racists while on tour). But through their art they helped break down racial stereotypes.

Only two major black jazz musicians made overtly political musical statements during the swing era. One was Billie Holiday, who sang the haunting anti-lynching song 'Strange Fruit'. The song was written by a white Jewish schoolteacher named Abel Meeropol.[16] The jazz writer Leonard Feather called the song 'the first significant protest in words and music, the first unmuted cry against racism'.[17] The lyrics to the song are:

LYNCH MOB TERROR

Southern trees bear a strange fruit,
Blood on the leaves and blood on the root,
Black body swinging in the Southern breeze,
Strange fruit hanging from the poplar trees.

Pastoral scene of the gallant South,
The bulging eyes and the twisted mouth,
Scent of magnolia sweet and fresh,
And the sudden smell of burning flesh!

Here is the fruit for the crows to pluck,
For the rain to gather, for the wind to suck,
For the sun to rot, for a tree to drop,
Here is a strange and bitter crop.

The other black jazz artist making overt statements was Duke Ellington. He said, 'I think a statement of social protest in the theatre should be made without saying it, and this calls for real craftsmanship'.[18] But pride in being black was central to Ellington's beliefs. His dream was to create a musical with an entirely black cast. In 1941 he achieved this with his show *Jump for Joy*. His pride in the finished product was obvious when he said, 'I've taken the "Uncle Tom" out of the theatre'.[19] Ellington also went on to produce *Black, Brown and Beige* in 1943 (see page 28), a musical based on the history of blacks in America.

Ellington also associated himself with the CPUSA. He played several CPUSA dances in the early 1930s. He also played numerous benefit concerts for the Scottsboro Boys, eight young black men falsely convicted of raping two white women and sentenced to death.[20]

It wasn't just black musicians who challenged racism. Many white musicians played an important role. Benny Goodman led one of the first integrated bands and refused to play to segregated audiences. Lionel Hampton, a black member of Goodman's band, remembers in a club one evening when a drunk stumbled over to their table and asked, 'Benny, what are you doing with all them niggers in your band?' 'If you say that again,' Goodman answered, 'I'll take this clarinet and bust you across the head with it.' The drunk backed off.[21]

There were also major battles to desegregate concert halls. In 1939 singer Marian Anderson was refused the use of Constitution Hall for a concert because she was black. A concert was hastily organised by anti-racists for her at the Lincoln Memorial Hall which drew 75,000 integrated fans and was a massive victory for the anti-racist movement.

The Great Depression, racism, and the wonderful music of Artie Shaw, Duke Ellington and Count Basie shaped Coltrane's formative years. These bandleaders forged the way for more complex and challenging music. Their breaches in the walls of racial segregation allowed the jazz musicians who followed to make even bolder political statements in their music, and the rumblings of this new musical revolution were already stirring in New York City.

Duke Ellington
Black, Brown and Beige (Columbia Records)

DUKE ELLINGTON

Ellington premiered the *Black, Brown and Beige* suite at Carnegie Hall on 23 January 1943. The composition was broken up into three sections. 'Black', the first section, contrasted the secular work song with the sacred and religious side of black life.

'Brown', the second section, drew its inspiration from the black heroes of the revolutionary wars. It is divided into two parts: the jangling 'West Indian Dance' celebrated the contribution the 545 black soldiers from Haiti made to the battle of Savannah during the American War of Independence; the second part, 'Emancipation Celebration', evokes the achievements of black troops in the American Civil War.

In the third section, 'Beige', Ellington comes right up to date. He portrays Harlem as a place of singing and dancing. But he also tries to show that Afro-Americans had other concerns – religion, education and advancement.

The concert and subsequent record were the first major musical works looking at Afro-American history and life. By playing at Carnegie Hall, Ellington had broken the colour bar of this classical concert venue. The $5,000 raised from the Carnegie Hall concert was donated to Russian war relief.

02 / Bebop

The entry of the US into the Second World War ushered in another exodus of blacks from the South to the Northern ghettos. Around 1.25 million migrated from the rural South to work in the war industries in the North and California. The impact on Northern cities and the West Coast was enormous. For example, in Los Angeles 100,000 new black defence workers poured into the city. Because of racist segregation in housing policies, blacks were forced to live in certain areas. The suburb of Watts was transformed from a semi-rural area into a suburban black ghetto.[1]

John Coltrane graduated from high school in 1943 and immediately left High Point to join his mother, aunt and cousin Mary in Philadelphia. They had moved there a year previously to find work in the wartime industries. Coltrane found work in a sugar refinery and later in a Campbell's soup factory. It was at this time that Coltrane bought his first alto saxophone. Unlike High Point, Philadelphia had a thriving black community. As well as jobs a-plenty, there were countless bars and clubs and theatres which showcased major stars both nationally and locally. The city was a melting pot of musical sounds. Major swing bands would regularly perform, but band leaders like Lionel Hampton and Louis Jordan were also creating a new sound which would be known as rhythm and blues. Coltrane was mesmerised by it all – he already hero-worshipped Johnny Hodges, the alto saxophone star of the Duke Ellington orchestra, and spent hour after hour trying to copy his sound.

At this time Coltrane was also accepted as a student at the Ornstein School of Music. The head of the school, Leo Ornstein, was born in Ukraine and moved to America in 1907. He was a virtuoso pianist whose experimental compositions aroused great controversy in the early part of the century. The young Coltrane was not only given traditional musical training but was also exposed to experimental classical music.

With America's entry into the Second World War, once again blacks were called on to do their 'duty'. Around 905,000 blacks enlisted into the army.[2] In 1945 Coltrane was called up and joined the US navy. He was stationed in Hawaii. When they discovered that he was an aspiring musician they assigned him to a black-only navy band – the Melody Masters. The band played to white audiences on the island. One navy paper report from one of the band's gigs stated, '[They] have done much to break down the racial barriers around the island.

Lovers of fine swing are not prejudiced against who gives it to them, and the Melody Masters gave fine swing'.[3] After leaving the navy Coltrane used his GI bonds to pay for more advanced music lessons at Philadelphia's Granoff Studios, where Dennis Sandole taught harmony and chord structures. Just as importantly, he began to study the music of Stravinsky and other great classical composers.

For those who found work in the new war industries their standard of living was better than it was in the South. But blacks still got the worst jobs and still found themselves living in rat-infested tenement blocks, and police harassment went on unabated. Coltrane was deeply shocked when, shortly after the war, his friend Nasseridine was clubbed to death by racist police officers.[4] Black troops returning from the war expected to be treated as heroes. The reality was different – many were set on by racist mobs and, in the South, lynchings went on with the complicity of the authorities. Writer James Baldwin summed up the deep sense of despair many blacks felt then when he wrote, 'The treatment accorded the Negro during the Second World War marks, for me, a turning point in the Negro's relationship to the US. To put it briefly and somewhat too simply, a certain hope died, a certain respect for white America faded'.[5]

Although it looked as though it was business as usual as far as the establishment was concerned, beneath the surface things were slowly changing. The coming together of thousands of black people in towns and cities did give them more confidence to fight back against racism. Blacks called for the Double V – victory against the Nazis and victory against racism in the US. In 1941 black union leader Philip Randolph, the head of the International Brotherhood, threatened to march on Washington if discrimination was not ended in the war industries. The New York and Chicago 'race riots' of 1943-44 also showed blacks were willing to fight back. In Chicago the Congress for Racial Equality (CORE) was founded in 1942. It was an outgrowth of Christian pacifist groups. An interracial organisation, it pursued racial equality through non-violent direct action methods. Borrowing heavily from the sit-down strike techniques developed by the CIO unions in the 1930s, CORE challenged segregation through sit-ins and picketings of restaurants and theatres in Chicago and other cities throughout the 1940s. Pressure from below forced President Roosevelt to formally ban segregation in the armed forces and war industries in 1941. Roosevelt also put pressure on Hollywood to include more black faces in its films. The studios hired Duke Ellington, Count Basie and Louis Armstrong. The US authorities were more than willing to use black jazz musicians for their needs.

Despite all the hardship the black ghettos were vibrant and alive. Blacks sought out and created their own entertainment and culture. Dance halls, clubs and theatres thrived. Although concert venues in the South remained segregated, many in the Northern cities began to allow mixed audiences.

The development of the long playing (LP) record at the end of the Second World War totally transformed the music industry. In musical terms its impact was even greater than that of the radio. Before the introduction of the LP, music was recorded on 78 rpm discs which only allowed a maximum of four minutes playing time. The development of LPs enabled jazz musicians to extend the length of compositions and also gave them a chance to show off a wide variety of songs on one record. Record sales rocketed. The main benefactors were the record companies which made massive profits. Sales of records rose from $3,000 million in 1940 to $11,000 million in 1950.[6]

The result was that commercial pressures and restrictions on musicians also increased. The growing popularity of jazz and other music forms meant that record companies and promoters fought harder and harder to control what the musicians played. However, compared to the pop, rock and soul artists who followed, jazz musicians were given far greater musical freedom. Even today record companies and promoters treat jazz music as a secondary market. This freedom gave the music more time to develop, which was denied to most other music forms.

It was still no picnic for jazz musicians. Countless stories are told by the jazz pioneers of the exploitation and racism that they faced at the hands of record companies. Two examples will suffice.

In the late 1930s Count Basie signed to MCA. It was the most expensive blunder of his life. When examining the contract closely, Basie discovered that it called for the band's exclusive services for three years. The $750 advance was the full payment for the 24 sides he had to record, and the money was to be shared out between his 26-piece band.

That worked out at less than $25 a player.[7] Fifteen years later Bob Weinstock, head of Prestige Records, offered to record the Mingus Trio for the paltry sum of $10 each, a free lunch and a little cocaine.[8] Would a record company have treated somebody like Bing Crosby in this way?

It wasn't just record companies that exploited jazz musicians. Club owners and concert venues made small fortunes out of touring jazz bands and with just a few notable exceptions musicians were poorly paid and treated with contempt.

By the 1940s swing had reached a musical cul de sac. Many musicians became frustrated by the limitations of playing in a large band, and looked for new and original ways of expression. Older members of the big swing bands accepted a degree of boredom and the brief solos this type of music offered them as a condition of working. But the younger generation, notably Gillespie and Parker, openly flouted the rules. Gillespie's reaction to the boredom of this daily routine was to play at a furious pace and to cram as many harmonic and melodic ideas as he could into the brief solo time allotted him. Also to the annoyance of his band leader, Cab Calloway, he spent the rest of the time playing practical jokes and clowning around!

Secondly, many large swing bands could not sustain themselves because so many musicians were conscripted into the armed forces. Swing remained as popular as ever but a new form of jazz began to develop – bebop.

Bebop revolutionised jazz. It differed from swing in two ways. Firstly, it is played by small groups in which the drummer and bassist are on a musical par with the horn and piano soloists. Secondly, bebop is much more complex music. It places greater influence on several rhythms playing at the same time. It is fast and frenetic, and improvisation lies at its heart. Bebop is a democratic music – it requires skilful interplay between the group, but it also highlights the individual musician's skills.

Those behind the bebop revolution included Charlie Parker, Dizzy Gillespie, Max Roach and Thelonious Monk. Swing bandleaders tended to come from middle class families, while the pioneers of bebop and all subsequent movements in jazz came mainly from working class backgrounds.[9] Interestingly, very few old time big band players made the move into bebop. It was a movement of the youth. Almost without exception all the major bebop artists were born between 1917 and 1924. This put them all in their early twenties during the formative years of the music. They were all young enough to want to put their own mark on the music, just like the young musical revolutionaries Louis Armstrong and Duke Ellington had put their stamp on jazz in the 1920s.

Bebop originated in New York. LeRoi Jones argues that beboppers saw themselves as 'self-conscious artists, not entertainers'.[10] They raised the quality of jazz from the level of dance music to that of chamber art. The bebop revolution of the early 1940s is inconceivable without the political upheavals brought about during the 1930s and the war. The period gave black Americans increased confidence – but it also brought them up against institutional racism, which stood between them and equality. The bebop revolution was as much political as it was musical. When Charlie Parker played his song 'Now is the Time' it was obvious to a lot of people what he meant – now is the time to end racism.

Dizzy Gillespie and Charlie Parker made a conscious point of hiring white musicians – George Wallington, Stan Levey and Red Rodney. Their very presence in a bebop band was a powerful statement – a deliberate breaching of artificial segregation barriers.

The confidence of the black and Latino jazz fans also came across in the clothes they wore. When Malcolm X was young he was a street hustler who loved jazz and dancing. In his autobiography he describes buying his first zoot suit:

> I was measured, and the young salesman picked off a rack a zoot suit that was just wild: sky blue pants 30 inches in the knee and angle-narrowed down to 12 inches at the bottom, and a long coat that pinched my waist and flared out below my knees... Then he said I ought to also buy a hat, and I did – blue with a feather in the four-inch brim. Then the store gave me another present: a long, thick lined gold plated chain that swung down lower than my coat hem. I was sold forever on credit.[11]

The clothes the beboppers wore set them apart from the rest of mainstream society. Parker had a penchant for English tweed suits, and Dizzy Gillespie wore a beret and had a goatee beard. Their clothes and attitude shocked the establishment.

In many ways the beboppers were the first punks! As Ross Russell, the biographer of Charlie Parker, observed:

> [Parker] could count his achievements with a certain measure of worldly pride. He was a high school dropout, professional musician, dabbler in drugs, a member of Local 627 of the American Federation of Musicians, married and a father to be – that August he celebrated his fifteenth birthday! [12]

Many beboppers hung around with those pushed to the fringes of society – poets, gays, artists, drug pushers and pimps. Many described themselves as 'beats', which was short for beatitude – the blessed downtrodden in society. As with most new and exciting art forms, bebop was condemned out of hand by most jazz critics. Some even claimed the music was anti-jazz! This was a criticism aimed at Coltrane when he once again revolutionised jazz 20 years later.

Bebop developed at a furious rate. This creativity was possible because of the environment it was performed in. Musicians from different bands would often meet up and jam with each other or hold musical duels. By jamming together musicians would share their musical knowledge and tricks with one another, and this allowed the music to continue developing. If a newcomer was confident enough he could get up on the bandstand and play with the giants of jazz.

Coltrane was discharged from the navy in 1946. He immediately returned to Philadelphia and immersed himself in the heady excitement of the new music and the blossoming bebop scene. Over the next 15 years the city was going to produce a new generation of jazz musicians who would follow in the wake of Coltrane – trumpeter Lee Morgan, saxophonist Archie Shepp, pianists McCoy Tyner and Bobby Timmons, organist Jimmy Smith, and bassists Jimmy Garrison and Reggie Workman.

During the mid to late 1940s Coltrane found work playing in a number of R&B bands, including those of King Kolax and Eddie 'Cleanhead' Vision. At the same time he honed his skills as a jazz musician. It was during this period that Coltrane shifted to the instrument that would become his mainstay – the tenor saxophone. Coltrane jammed with Charlie Parker on several occasions and told the jazz magazine *Down Beat* magazine years later, 'The first time I heard Bird [Parker] play, it hit me right between the eyes'.[13] Coltrane also met Miles Davis for the first time in 1947. Their paths would cross again eight years later when Coltrane joined the Miles Davis Quintet. The clubs and dance halls in which the young Coltrane cut his teeth were laboratories of musical experimentation. In September 1949 he got his first major break – a regular place in Dizzy Gillespie's band. For the next 18 months he toured and played in the band. At this point in his musical career Coltrane was just copying other musicians' styles. He admitted as much in an interview in *Down Beat*:

I was playing in cliches and trying to learn tunes that were hip, so I could play with the guys that could play them. Earlier, when I had first heard Bird, I wanted to be identified with him…to be consumed by him. But underneath I really wanted to be myself. You can only play so much of another man.[14]

Music still remained one of the few avenues open to blacks to express themselves. Whatever their talents, the vast majority of blacks were denied the opportunity to go to college, run businesses or become politicians. McCoy Tyner tells the story of how one night Parker met two scientists in a nightclub. For two hours he debated with them about the dialectic in nature. One of the scientists asked Parker what university he was taught at. He just laughed – he hadn't even finished his schooling.[15]

The bebop stars were great musicians, adored by jazz fans, but as soon as they climbed off the bandstand the reality of racism hit them in the face. Things were just as bad as they were in the 1930s. Drummer and band leader Art Blakey described what it was like touring in the US:

> We travelled through the South all day and we had a pocket full of money, but we couldn't get a glass of water, and if you did, they'd sell it to you for a dollar a glass. And it would be as hot as panther piss.[16]

Charlie Parker (Bird) found his own unique way of fighting back when he and his band arrived in St Louis to play the suitably named Plantation Club. He found that he was expected to use the rear entrance and play to a white-only crowd. When Bird tried to use the front entrance management blocked his way.

Bird was determined to make an issue of it. He went around to the back tables where the musicians were relaxing after a rehearsal, asking each man if he had drunk from the glass in front of him. Receiving an affirmative answer, Charlie carefully broke each glass, explaining that management would of course not expect any of its regular customers to use the same glass as a black man. After a number of glasses were smashed the club's owner, a well known St Louis gangster, arrived, and a fight was only narrowly avoided.[17] The first time Charlie Parker was called Mr Parker was when he was touring in Sweden.

Several of those connected to the bebop revolution hung out with the Communist Party. Charlie Parker, Miles Davis, Max Roach and Charles Mingus all played benefits for the CPUSA. Even as late as 1951 jazz musicians such as Miles Davis, Sonny Rollins and J J Johnson all played benefits for the Labour Youth League, a front for the CPUSA.[18]

For a brief period Dizzy Gillespie even joined the Communist Party. He recalled:

We played all the Communist dances. The Communists held a lot of them in Brooklyn, the Bronx and Manhattan. At those Communist dances they were always trying to recruit you. As a matter of fact, I signed one of those cards. I was a card-carrying Communist because it was directly associated with my work.[19]

Bebop was never as popular as swing. There are several reasons why this was so. At the height of the bebop revolution in 1942, the American Federation of Musicians imposed a recording ban on musicians. The ban was widely supported by musicians because it was an attempt to get decent royalty payments for radio and jukebox plays. It was in effect a strike, and it lasted until 1944 when the big record labels finally gave some concessions and signed new contracts. The strike meant that some of the most exciting bebop music was never recorded.

But the musicians' strike wasn't the main reason bebop remained a minority music. Both black and white audiences preferred the 'modern ballad' singers like Frank Sinatra, Perry Como and Bing Crosby. Their music was far more accessible than bebop – the stress was very much on entertainment and showmanship. Even more importantly, it had the backing of the major record companies. The black music that was really pulling in the crowds was Chicago rhythm and blues, and the jump bands of Cab Calloway. By the late 1940s promoters were refusing to hire large bands. They were already glimpsing the possibilities of turning black rhythm and blues into the goldmine called rock and roll.

*Miles Davis on the cover of **Birth of the Cool***

03 / Cool

The end of the Second World War ushered in a new period of economic growth and stability in the US – the long boom had begun. This unprecedented level of growth would last until the 1970s, and workers' standard of living continued to rise throughout this period. It was not just a question of income. A wide range of consumer goods, televisions, cars, record players and fridges became affordable to a large number of working class people – both black and white.

Bebop continued to be the dominant form of jazz throughout the late 1940s. But by the early 1950s the music began to stagnate. Musicians and audiences alike became bored with it. One of those looking to create a new sound was Miles Davis. He was one of the young stars of the bebop era. Davis had played on and off with Charlie Parker. But in 1948 Davis launched his solo career. He moved away from the bebop sound and recorded with a nine-piece band. Eight of the tracks were originally issued on 78s. It wasn't until 1957 that all the tracks were brought together on one album titled *Birth of the Cool*.

The music was a move away from the total improvisation and fierce rhythms of bebop. Davis developed a more 'laid back' and orchestral style of playing. He stripped jazz away from its roots in the blues and pushed it towards a sound that had far more in common with European classical music. The critics labelled the music as 'cool' or 'West Coast jazz', because most of the musicians who played this kind of music were based on the West Coast of America. During the early 1950s Davis's sound spawned a host of imitators.

There is always a danger of trying to pin labels on musical styles. Music categories are usually the invention of music critics and not something with which many musicians identify. Some musicians' work is hard to categorise. For instance, it is impossible to label the music of Duke Ellington, Thelonious Monk or Charles Mingus. But nevertheless these basic categories (swing, bebop and cool) are a useful tool in describing the development of jazz.

For a brief period cool jazz became fantastically popular. Almost every single Hollywood film of the period seems to have a cool jazz soundtrack. Cool also had a big influence with those closely associated with what became known as the 'beat generation', Jack Kerouac and Allen Ginsberg. This helped popularise the music among a new generation of white youth in America and Europe.

White musicians like Chet Baker, Stan Getz and Gerry

Mulligan dominated cool. They all had one thing in common – they were trained in classical European music. Dave Brubeck, one of the key figures, was often quoted saying, 'I want to classicise jazz.' In effect Brubeck wanted to divorce jazz from its black roots. The only prominent black musician playing the music, Miles Davis, would later repudiate the style. As a school of music it was sterile and left no lasting influence on jazz.

However, cool music did have one positive impact. It opened up the beauty of jazz to a large number of young white kids, many of who went on to discover Ellington, Parker and the other key figures. A similar thing happened in the 1960s when the Rolling Stones played a form of the blues. Many of their fans moved on to explore the real blues tradition. (One of the greatest blues players, John Lee Hooker, is quoted as saying, 'The Rolling Stones were the best thing that ever happened to my career.')

Although the economy was booming, for most black jazz musicians the first half of the 1950s was tough. Many found it increasingly hard to financially support themselves playing music, audiences were dwindling, and concert promoters were not prepared to book bebop bands. Crooners like Frank Sinatra and Dean Martin became all the rage. Both trombone player J J Johnston and Charles Mingus ended up working in the post office in the early 1950s, and McCoy Tyner ended up driving a taxicab in Manhattan for a living.[1]

John Coltrane was more fortunate. He spent the early 1950s earning his living playing jazz and jump music in small clubs and bars. Coltrane's second major break came when alto saxophonist Johnny Hodges asked him to join his touring band. Hodges had played in the Duke Ellington band since the 1930s, but he left in 1953 and decided to set up his own group. The Hodges band played mostly Ellington material. For the first time in his life Coltrane was making a living playing music. He earned $250 a week – a tidy sum in those days.[2]

It was around this time that Coltrane became addicted to heroin. The consequences were disastrous. John Williams, the band's bassist, recalls, '[Coltrane] would be sitting in his chair, holding his horn but not moving his fingers. The sax was still in his mouth but he was not playing. This happened night after night'.[3] Hodges sacked Coltrane. During the 1940s and 1950s a whole host of jazz musicians would fall under the 'dragon's spell' (see page 50).

The massive economic boom of the 1950s and 1960s concealed deep-seated tensions in US society. By 1948 the world was divided into two camps – one under the control of Stalin's Russia, and the other under the influence of the US and its Western allies. Tensions increased when the US got involved in the Korean War. The Cold War had begun, and it was used as an excuse to attack Communists in the US. The Taft-Hartley law required trade unions to purge Communist officials from their ranks. By the mid-1950s the CPUSA was almost wiped out, and literally thousands of trade union militants were thrown out of their jobs.

Senator Joe McCarthy's House Un-American Activities Committee (HUAC) waged an unrelenting war on what he described as 'Communist infiltration' of Hollywood and the entertainment industry. The HUAC crippled Hollywood. A survey conducted by the Writers Guild found that films dealing with social problems decreased from 20.9 percent in 1947 to less than 4 percent by 1954.[4] Blockbusters, musicals and war films dominated the cinema, the vast majority of which reinforced the 'American way of life'.

It wasn't only Hollywood that was affected – the music industry also suffered at the hands of the HUAC. Frank Sinatra, one of the biggest singing stars of the 1940s, was released from his film contract and nearly dropped by his record label after he was accused by the HUAC of support-ing Communist front organisations.[5] Record companies ruthlessly policed what they released and dropped artists with left leanings.

Any socialist prepared to make a stand was brutally dealt with. Paul Robeson was proof of that. Robeson broke the mould. He was an incredibly gifted black American. He was one of a handful of blacks to gain entrance into univer-sity. He graduated from Columbia University with a law degree in 1923. He played four different sports at national level and was twice named All-American football player of the year. But he dropped it all to become a singer and actor. He starred in countless plays, he was one of the first black film icons and his beautiful deep baritone bass voice made him an international star.

Like thousands he had been radicalised by the political events of the 1930s. He became a vocal opponent of racism and supported the CPUSA. Robeson was called the 'Black Stalin' by the press during the height of the McCarthy witch-hunt and was forced to appear before the HUAC in 1956, where he delivered a slamming defence of his beliefs, saying, 'You want to shut up every Negro who has the courage to stand up and fight for the rights of his people.'

When the HUAC asked him why he didn't move to Russia, he answered, 'Because my father was a slave, and my people died to build this country, and I am going to stay here and have my part just like you. And no fascist minded people will drive me from it. Is that clear?'[6]

The government withdrew Robeson's passport. Blacklisted and unable to tour, his career was in tatters. Robeson died a broken man in 1976. He was an inspiration for many black and white people. But what happened to him was also a reminder to many of the dangers of speaking out.

Paul Robeson speaks out

Drugs

CHARLIE 'YARDBIRD' PARKER

John Coltrane was one in a long line of jazz musicians, which included Charlie Parker, Art Blakey, Bill Evans, Sonny Rollins, Bud Powell and Miles Davis, who became addicted to heroin. Many jazz critics claim that heroin addiction among jazz musicians was just a fad – a fashion statement.

It is a sad but undeniable fact that many jazz musicians took heroin in a vain hope that it would give them greater creative powers. However, for Miles Davis and many others the use of heroin was explicitly tied to a deep sense of frustration and alienation with the American way of life.

In 1949 Davis made his first trip overseas for a week-long festival in Paris. There he was treated like a superstar. On his return to New York, his new found sense of confidence began to crumble – he couldn't find work and began to be more aware of racism. He recalled in his autobiography, 'I started to notice things I'd never noticed before – "political stuff" – what was happening to black people.' Before long Davis turned to heroin to escape the pain. He adds in his autobiography, 'To realise you don't have any power to make things different is a bitch. I lost my sense of discipline, lost my sense of control over my life, and I started to drift.' Drug abuse had become a way of escaping the hardships of the real world.

04 / Hard bop and Coltrane's big break

By the late 1950s McCarthyism was on the decline, the Korean War was over, and the grip of the right in America began to loosen.

On 1 December 1955 a black woman, Rosa Parks, refused to give up her seat on a bus to a white person. Her arrest sparked off the year-long Montgomery bus boycott. The protest forced the bus companies to desegregate the buses. The victory inspired a wave of sit-ins and boycotts all over the South. The Montgomery bus boycott was the beginning of a long and bloody struggle to break the Jim Crow racism of the South. It was not the National Association for the Advancement of Colored People (NAACP) that led this movement – its own conservative politics and its fear of a McCarthyite witch hunt left it paralysed. Instead the church provided the base for an alternative movement and an alternative organisation, the Southern Christian Leadership Conference (SCLC). The SCLC was led by Dr Martin Luther King Jr. King preached mass non-violent resistance. Thousands of black and white activists flocked to join King and the civil rights movement.

The victory in Montgomery was hard fought. In the run up to the campaign civil rights workers and blacks in general faced violent opposition. In early spring 1955 Gus Courts, the head of the NAACP in Belzoni, Mississippi, was critically wounded in a shotgun attack. The reason? He refused to surrender his right to vote. In May of the same year a black minister in Belzoni who was organising a black voter registration drive was murdered while driving his car. In August a black man was shot outside a courthouse in the middle of the day and in front of several witnesses. The victim, Lamar Smith, had been actively working to defeat a county supervisor who was trying to block blacks registering to vote. The judge involved in the case bragged that no white man was willing to testify against another in the murder of a black man.

Two weeks later the most infamous of these killings was perpetrated in Mississippi. The murder had no apparent connection with politics – it was an out and out lynching whose only purpose was to terrorise the black community. Emmett Till, a 14 year old boy from Chicago, was accused of having 'wolf-whistled' a white woman. He was kidnapped from his grandfather's home in the middle of the night, pistol-whipped, stripped naked and shot. His body was then barb-wired to a cotton gin fan and dumped in the Tallahatchie River. The Emmett Till case became a rallying cry for the movement. The NAACP charged that Mississippi 'has decided to maintain white supremecy by mudering children'. This level of repression makes the resistance in Montgomery and what was to follow even more remarkable and inspiring.

John Coltrane's big break came the same year as Rosa Parks refused to give her seat up on the bus in Montgomery. In 1955 Miles Davis asked him to join his band. Coltrane was only a few months younger than Davis, but whereas Davis had been recording since 1945 and had featured with all the jazz greats, Coltrane was virtually unknown. Davis, never one to downplay his role in discovering Coltrane, wrote:

> The critic Whitney Balliet said not long after Trane [Coltrane] and I were playing that Coltrane had a 'dry, unplanned tone that sets Davis off, like a rough mounting for a fine stone'. But before long, Trane was much more than that. After a while he was a diamond himself, and I knew it, and everybody else who heard him knew it too.[1]

The Miles Davis Quintet quickly established a major following. The band's last five albums for the Prestige record label (*Miles*, *Cookin'*, *Relaxin'*, *Workin'* and *Steamin'*) have endured as some of the most beautiful albums of the 1950s. They restored the blues and improvisation into jazz. Sly Johnson, composer and pianist, remembers when the quintet first came to Los Angeles: 'It blew everybody out of the water. It destroyed West Coast jazz overnight.' What set their music apart from all the rest was Davis's sparse, introspective playing and Coltrane's blustering sound. The Miles Davis Quintet had everything. It played standards like 'Bye Bye Blackbird', 'My Funny Valentine' and 'Surrey with the Fringe on Top' which gave it popular appeal, as well as more challenging pieces. The quintet was hailed by the music press as the 'saviour of jazz'. The Miles Davis Quintet was a break from the music of cool.

It wasn't just Davis who spotted the talent of Coltrane. Bob Weinstock, the chief of Prestige Records, began to take note. He approached Coltrane and asked him to sign a three-year contract to record under his own name. Coltrane did sign the contract but his modesty meant that he did not feel confident to record any album with his own band for the next year and a half. But in the next year and a half Coltrane recorded six albums with the Miles Davis Quintet on the Prestige label and one for Columbia. He also became an integral part of the Prestige label, recording a number of sessions led by other band leaders including Paul Chambers, Johnny Griffin, Hank Mobley, Max Waldron and a host of others. Coltrane soon became, in the words of pianist Tommy Flanagan, one of the 'one take masters' – a musician who could walk into a studio and know through instinct what the band leader required.

The Miles Davis Quintet won almost every jazz award going. But things were far from perfect in the band. Coltrane's playing provoked a mixed reaction from the critics – some obviously loved his style of playing while others complained that his solos were too long and that his 'sound' was too coarse. But there was a much more serious problem. Davis, in his usual inimitable way, explained the mess Coltrane was in: 'He'd be playing in clothes that looked like he had slept in them for days, all wrinkled up and dirty and shit. Then he'd be standing up there when he wasn't nodding [off] – picking his nose and sometimes eating it'.[2] Coltrane's drug problems continued to haunt him. According to the jazz writer Ashley Kahn, in October 1956:

> Davis exploded at a date at New York's Cafe Bohemia, berating Coltrane for his slovenly appearance and tardiness. According to Davis, the saxophonist was too much in a stupor to respond with anything but silence. Exasperated, the diminutive trumpeter slapped the smaller sideman in the head, and slugged him in the stomach. Coltrane still offered no resistance. A nonplussed Thelonious Monk, who had witnessed the one-sided argument, stepped in and urged the saxophonist to quit and join his band.[3]

Coltrane took the opportunity to get his life together. He came off heroin and started playing with the great jazz pianist Thelonious Monk. The interplay between Monk and Coltrane was amazing. The jazz critic Ira Gitler claims in the sleevenotes to *Thelonious Monk and John Coltrane*, 'Although the group remained together for only a half year, those of us who heard it will never forget the experience... The music was kinetic and hypnotic.

THELONIOUS MONK

J J Johnson has compared it to the mid-1940s union of Charlie Parker and Dizzy Gillespie – praise indeed'. Monk gave Coltrane the space to experiment with his playing. On tracks like 'Trinkle, Trinkle' and 'Nutty', Coltrane's saxophone sounds more like a cello being bowed. It was also during this time that Monk began to urge Coltrane to develop a playing style using groups of notes rather than one note at a time. Coltrane explained the impact of Monk: '[He] showed me how to make two or three notes at one time on tenor...he just looked at my horn and "felt" the mechanics of what had to be done to get this effect'.[4]

It was this sound that Coltrane developed, with the help of Monk, that would revolutionise jazz music. Some of the music Monk and Coltrane made together can be heard on three excellent studio albums – *Thelonious Himself*, *Thelonious Monk with John Coltrane* and *Monk's Music* and a poorly recorded live album *Live at the Five Spot Discovery*. They may only have been together for a six-month period, but Monk had a massive influence on Coltrane's unique sound.

The Miles Davis Quintet were not creating music in a vacuum. They were part of a second school of jazz music which developed during the 1950s – it was known as hard bop (soul jazz and funky jazz were other titles given to the music). Throughout the late 1950s Coltrane recorded albums with many of the great hard bop players including Gene Ammons, Sonny Rollins, Donald Byrd and Red Garland. Theirs was a music that was proud to be black and was clearly inspired by the civil rights movement. It was also a reaction by black musicians against cool. This new style of jazz tried to breathe new life into bebop. It drew inspiration from gospel music and restored the art of improvisation. Most importantly the blues once again became central to the music.

Art Blakey described hard bop as 'the back to the roots movement'. Between 1957 and 1962 there were literally hundreds of album and song titles which reflected the growing sense of pride in being black. Here are just a few: Sonny Rollins, *Airegin* (Nigeria spelt backwards); Julian 'Cannonball' Adderley, *Something Else* (what black people and their music are); Lou Donalson's, *The Time is Right* (for liberation); and Max Roach's *It's Time* (which was short for now is the time for liberation).[5] The titles of the songs and albums were oblique enough to get past the record company executives and most music reviewers, but as Art Blakey said, 'They were obvious to those who needed to know'.[6]

Another organisation that began to have a minor influence on jazz at this time was Elijah Muhammad's Nation of Islam. The cover of Art Blakey's album *Moanin'* (which meant the prayer of a black worshipper) shows a striking image of Blakey shaven headed, suited and wearing a bow tie. This was the standard dress of any male member of the Nation of Islam. The Nation of Islam was the largest black nationalist organisation in the US in the 1950s. A TV documentary programme, *The Hate That Hate Produced*, estimated that its membership was 250,000.[7] This was a massive exaggeration, but nevertheless the organisation had a serious influence in black communities. It grew into a formidable force because it promoted self-reliance, clean living and black pride. It drew into its ranks two notable figures – Cassius Clay (Muhammad Ali) and Malcolm X. Many black people were drawn to the Nation of Islam because it talked of standing up against racism. But the organisation remained aloof from the struggle waged by King in the South.

The civil rights movement had a profound influence on Coltrane. On one of his first solo albums, entitled *Coltrane* (Prestige) and recorded in 1957, Coltrane recorded the track 'Bakai'. 'Bakai' was written by Cal Massey and is dedicated to the memory of Emmet Till. Bakai is the Arabic word for cry.

It is rightly claimed that Coltrane was the most influential player in modern jazz. That achievement is even more remarkable given that it was packed into a single decade of music making. Almost exactly ten years separate the first record as leader, *Dakar* in 1957, and the anguished curtain call of *Expression*, made just weeks before his death in 1967. The early Coltrane-led albums recorded by Prestige, including *Dakar*, *Coltrane*, *Lush Life*, *Bahia* and *Traneing In*, are a mixed bag. The line-ups continually change as Coltrane looks for a permanent band to build his ideas around. They clearly demonstrate an artist attempting to find his own sound and push back the boundaries of hard bop. There are also several examples of his high speed virtuoso playing and a dazzling comand of harmonic nuance. But it is on his ballad solos, especially the track 'Violets for Your Furs' from the album *Coltrane*, that you can really begin to hear a soloist with the confidence of Armstrong or Parker begining to shine through.

In 1957 Coltrane also recorded his only album for Blue Note, *Blue Train*, which today remains one of his most commercially popular albums. In many ways it was a transitional album for Coltrane as much of it harks back to Coltrane's time in the Miles Davis Quintet. However, the title track gives some flavour of the direction in which Coltrane was going to take his music. There is also one other key factor about the Blue Note session. Prestige had a reputation for recording jam sessions and only making one take. Blue Note on the other hand paid for rehearsal time, provided much greater studio time and prided itself on its finished product – that is why when Coltrane was asked what was his favourite album he would often reply *Blue Train*.

Davis in the meantime had become bored of the musical cliches and old style bebop formulae that became the mainstay of hard bop. As a direct result of and inspired by the bleak Louis Malle thriller *L'Ascenseur Pour L'echafaud* (*Lift to the Scaffold*) Davis began to develop a new sound, 'modal jazz'. Malle had asked Davis to write and perform the sound track to the film. To create the darkness and suspense in the film Davis began to revisit the question of composition. His normal blistering tempos (a sound rooted in the hard bop canon) were slowed down and Davis began experimenting with time signatures. Not only did he employ the simple straight ahead 4/4 – he introduced more unusual time signatures such as waltzlike 3/4 and 6/8 metres. Without doubt *L'Ascenseur Pour L'echafaud* is a marvellous and often neglected Davis record.

In the months after Davis had kicked Coltrane out of his band he had managed to persuade the alto saxophone player Cannonball Adderley to join him. By late 1957 Davis asked

Coltrane to rejoin his group. He wanted two saxophone players in his band creating a textured and layered sound. It was a very different Coltrane who returned to the Davis band – Coltrane was clean of drugs and had developed a unique, fiery sound. It was also a Coltrane who had undgone a further deepening of his religious beliefs. Davis now had a sextet. He put his ideas into practice and produced the enduring *Milestones*.

Record companies were now eager to snap up Coltrane. At the end of 1968 Coltrane joined Atlantic Records on a one-year $7,000 contract plus a Lincoln Continental car! The contract also allowed him to continue to record with the Miles band. Atlantic Records was a leading independent label better known for its sucess in the R&B market with artists like Ray Charles and the Chords than with jazz musicians. In fact jazz was regarded by the company as a sideline market. Interestingly, the company was to make more money over the years from its jazz back catalogue. But just like Blue Note the company did give Coltrane paid practice time, ample recording time and his own inhouse engineer. However, as was standard practice for jazz labels in the 1950s and 1960s, both Atlantic Records and Prestige recorded Coltrane's surplus material and continued to release further albums by the artist long after he had moved on to pastures new. This way Atlantic was able to piggyback each one of Coltrane's albums released on Impulse! during the 1960s with its own.

In the spring of 1959 Coltrane played on two of the greatest jazz albums ever – Miles Davis's *Kind of Blue* and his own

Giant Steps. The album notes that accompany *Kind of Blue* begin:

> Art does not develop at a neat uniform rate. There are periods when it seems to be stagnating, and short ones when it appears to be striding forward in seven league boots.[8]

Well, when Davis recorded *Kind of Blue* he definitely had his boots on. It is one of the seminal recordings in the history of American music. The compositions are of exquisite beauty. Davis and Coltrane's improvisational freedom is combined with the subtlety of chamber music and the swing of jazz. Pianist Bill Evans explained what made these recordings so amazing:

> Miles conceived these settings only hours before the recording date, and arrived with sketches which indicated to the group what was to be played. Therefore you will hear something close to spontaneity in these performances. The group had never played these pieces before the recordings.[9]

Each track on the album is a classic. Just like *Milestones*, Davis and the band used modes as a basis for improvisation rather than chord changes. Coltrane explained in one interview the process that was going on in the studio, 'Miles was moving to the use of fewer and fewer chord changes in songs. He used tunes with free flowing lines and chordial direction.

This approach allowed the soloist the choice of playing chor-dially or melodically'.[10]

The track 'All Blues' is a variation of an old jazz theme. But Davis and the band use a Moorish backdrop over which each soloist plays. This enables each player to sustain and build on the mood of his predecessor. Likewise on the song 'Freddie Freeloader' the music is stripped down to its most basic elements. Coltrane's solo is spellbinding and adds a haunting quality to the music. The key track on the album for Coltrane was 'So What', in which he takes the first two saxophone solos. McCoy Tyner explained to the author of this book that it was in this session that Coltrane learnt to pare down his playing to the simplest level in order to focus on his own increasingly complex harmonic ideas.

On his solo album *Giant Steps*, Coltrane reached the ulti-mate in harmonic invention by stacking up chords on top of those normally played. This gave him an almost unlimited number of scales and patterns on which to play. The effect was mind blowing. Instead of single notes he created what one critic called 'sheets of sound'.[11] This style of playing was something Coltrane experimented with when he played with Thelonious Monk. This can best be heard on the title track and 'Countdown'. Every song on the album (with the exception of 'Spiral') has become a mainstay of the modern jazz book. If Coltrane had never made another album after *Giant Steps* he would still be in the jazz hall of fame. Finally in 1960 Coltrane left the Miles Davis Quintet for good.

The recording of **Blue Train**. *Photograph by Francis Wolff*

Abbey Lincoln, Max Roach, Charlie Mingus and Sonny Rollins

05 / Standing out against the stream

Mingus and I discussed how angry we both were about
social conditions. It was the natural reaction to the
societal ills we had to deal with... He knew I felt like
he did. His 'Fables of Faubus' and my 'Freedom Suite'
– the point is we were both thinking along these lines.
Mingus, me and Roach – activists trying to address
some of these social ills.

Sonny Rollins[1]

Four musicians in the late 1950s and 1960s – Sonny Rollins,
Max Roach, Abbey Lincoln and Charles Mingus – made
albums that overtly supported Martin Luther King's civil
rights movement.

Sonny Rollins

Like John Coltrane, Sonny Rollins was a jazz musician who learnt his trade with the stars of bebop. When in 1956 Rollins released *Tenor Madness* (Coltrane also played on this album) and *Saxophone Colossus* he established himself as one of the great saxophone players of all time. Two years later Rollins recorded the album *Freedom Now*. The meaning behind the title of the album was obvious to everyone.

He included this statement on the sleeve notes: 'America is deeply rooted in Negro culture: its colloquialisms, its humour and its music. How ironic that the Negro, who more than any other people can claim America's culture as his own, is being persecuted and repressed, that the Negro, who has exemplified the humanities in his very existence, is being rewarded with inhumanity'.[2]

To many readers today the statement may appear tame. But it is worth remembering that up until that point no other jazz musician had made such an overt political statement on the sleeve of their records. Despite Rollins's fame, Riverside, the record company, deleted the album almost immediately. They claimed that it did not sell well. There is no evidence that the album sold any worse than any other Rollins album. It was subsequently re-released under the new title *Shadow Waltz* – named after the second shortest track on the album!

Charles Mingus

Charles Mingus was one of the most innovative jazz musicians of the 20th century. A pioneering bassist, bandleader and composer, Mingus penned over 300 works spanning gutbucket gospel, modern big band jazz and free jazz. He was also an uncompromising opponent of racism. Many of his compositions openly supported the civil rights movement.

One of Mingus's most powerful pieces is the song 'Fables of Faubus'. First recorded in 1959, it was about the white racist governor of Arkansas, Orville Faubus. During the campaign to desegregate schools in Arkansas, Faubus stood symbolically in a school entrance to bar black school children from entering. Another composition included 'Haitian Fight Song' which was originally written in tribute to the Haitian revolutionary Toussaint L'Ouverture. Mingus was often quoted saying it could just as easily have been called 'African-American Fight Song'.

Another track, 'Don't Let It Happen Here', was an extended piece written in the early 1960s. Mingus had heard from Eric Dolphy (who would later collaborate with Coltrane) about prison camps in the South where civil rights protesters were incarcerated behind electric barbed wire fences. The image was not lost on Mingus, who began with a recital based on the famous anti-Nazi statement by Pastor Niemöller:

One day they came and they took the Communists,
And I said nothing because I was not a Communist.
Then one day they burned the Catholic churches,
And I said nothing because I was born a Protestant.

One day they came and took the unionists,
And I said nothing because I was not a unionist.
One day they came and they took away the people of the Jewish faith,
And I said nothing because I had no faith left.
Then one day they came and took me,
And I could say nothing because I was as guilty as they were, for not speaking out and saying that all men have a right to freedom.
Oh lord, don't let it happen here...

Mingus's political stance put him in conflict with record companies and club owners. Even though Mingus was for a brief period a card-carrying member of the CPUSA, he fought his battles against the system and racism in his own individualistic way. So, for instance, when a racist union official ripped off jazz musicians in New York, Mingus got organised. He put on a yellow hunter's outfit, got himself a few bodyguards and armed himself with a shotgun. When he arrived at the union meeting the official had a quick change of heart.[3]

Mingus once said, 'I always thought that no matter what kind of work people did, they should involve themselves totally with all the discrimination they ran into. I remember once in Yugoslavia we played 'Faubus' and 'Remember Rockefeller at Attica', and this US Embassy cat came running up and told me not to play songs with titles like that'.[4]

Mingus defied that man from the embassy and that is exactly how he lived his life – as an uncompromising fighter against racism.

Max Roach and Abbey Lincoln

Max Roach is one of the most influential drummers in the history of jazz. He was Charlie Parker's sidekick and, as stated earlier, he supported a number of CPUSA-initiated benefit concerts in the late 1940s and early 1950s. He played at and encouraged other musicians like Charlie Mingus and Roy Porter to attend Camp Unity. Camp Unity was a racially integrated summer camp organised by the CPUSA in the 1940s and early 1950s. Drummer Roy Porter recalled what the camp was like: 'The people there were all talking about racial equality, and I must admit I didn't hear one derogatory remark or see an incident while I was there'.[5]

When King began organising the civil rights movement Roach threw himself into the struggle, organising and playing benefits for the Southern Christian Leadership Conference (SCLC). During the late 1950s and early 1960s Roach released a number of albums that charted the struggle for civil rights. The first was *Deeds Not Words* (1958).

The second was the seminal album *We Insist! Freedom Now Suite* (1960). The artwork for the album depicted a group of young black men sitting at a white-only lunch counter. Not only did it openly declare its support for the activists involved in the protests, it was the first ever jazz album to openly depict the civil rights movement – in fact it is hard to recall any mainstream album of any genre that came out before *We Insist!* whose cover made such a bold statement. The singer on the album was Abbey Lincoln (who was at that time Max Roach's wife). Her vocal performance is one of the most convincing vehicles of black American experience since Billie Holiday. *We Insist! Freedom Now Suite* has had an incalculable influence on jazz music. But Abbey Lincoln paid a high price for her political stance. For over a decade after recording that album not one single US record company would sign her up.

Max followed *We Insist! Freedom Now* by the albums *Members, Don't Get Weary* (1960), *It's Time* (1962) and *Speak Brother Speak* (1962). More and more of Max's music began to return to the gospel music sung by the civil rights movement. Also, he became interested in African rhythm and drum patterns, a move that predated the free jazz movement by several years. Max also rejected the term jazz music for the term 'I play music'. It was a serious attempt to get his work taken seriously as art and not just mere entertainment. Also as he rightly points out, 'Why when I use so many different styles of music should I allow it to be categorised?' The Art Ensemble of Chicago put it a different way: 'We prefer to call it Great Black Music – it's great, it's black and it is music'.[6]

The political stance of Lincoln, Mingus, Roach and Rollins inspired a new generation of jazz musicians who were influenced by the Black Power movement, and who would also fall under the spell of John Coltrane.

06 / The Classic Quartet

'My Favourite Things', the Rogers and Hammerstein waltz, is best known as the song sung by Julie Andrews in the movie *The Sound of Music*. Coltrane recorded the track in 1960 and transformed this pretty tune into a grand, symphonic statement. 'My Favourite Things' was a song Coltrane played throughout his career. The album of the same name sold more than 50,000 copies during the first year of its release. This was phenomenal. A best-selling jazz album would usually sell about 5,000 copies at that time. Only Miles Davis sold more records. Listening to the many different recordings of the song by the quartet gives the listener a great feel for how the band was always changing musical direction.

Another factor that made *My Favourite Things* stand out was that it showcased Coltrane playing the soprano saxophone (Coltrane had been playing the soprano at live concerts and had also played it on his album *The Avant Garde* which was recorded several months before *My Favourite Things* but that album did not see the light of day until 1966). The soprano saxophone is an instrument with a very disctictive range – it

has an ability to emit a rich, hypnotic sound. This clearly suited Coltrane's interest in Eastern musical scales. Coltrane's search for new melodies led him to study even more. He informed one journalist, 'Most recently I've been listening to folk tunes and been trying to find some meaning in that. I feel that basically the music should be dedicated to the goodness in people, the good things in life...folk tunes usually spring from the simplest things... maybe I can work on this, listen to them and learn to combine what's done around the world with what I feel here'.[1]

In all, Coltrane recorded seven albums in the space of just two years for Atlantic Records. This prolific output would continue for the rest of his life as he continued to push back the boundaries of jazz. He also spent the time at Atlantic Records looking for a band that could develop his musical ideas. He went through several different musical line-ups, eventually settling on McCoy Tyner (piano), Elvin Jones (drums) and Jimmy Garrison (bass). The John Coltrane Quartet was born. It would remain intact until late 1965. Each member of the band contributed their own unique sound to the music.

McCoy Tyner was born in Philadelphia in 1938. He first met Coltrane in 1957 at a time when the saxophonist was withdrawing from his drug addiction. Tyner remembered:

'I used to sit on the porch of his mother's house and talk to him. Then he went back with Miles in the late 1950s, but we made a verbal commitment that I would join his band whenever he formed it.'[2] Tyner added a very spiritual quality to the quartet – his playing evokes power and thunder, but never loses its lyricism and melody.

Elvin Jones was born in 1927, in Pontiac, Michigan. He was the youngest of three brothers (with Hank and Thad) who all made careers playing jazz. After moving to New York, Jones quickly established himself as a great drummer, playing and recording with Miles Davis, J J Johnson and Sonny Rollins. Elvin was one of the strongest, wildest drummers in the world. His complex drumming patterns were pathbreaking. He established himself as an intense bebop drummer before going on to add new and complex drumming patterns to the rhythmic language of bop.

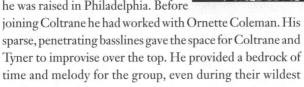

The final member was Jimmy Garrison. Born in Miami in 1937, he was raised in Philadelphia. Before joining Coltrane he had worked with Ornette Coleman. His sparse, penetrating basslines gave the space for Coltrane and Tyner to improvise over the top. He provided a bedrock of time and melody for the group, even during their wildest moments.

John Coltrane was not a 'natural born genius' somehow sprung fully formed, divinely inspired and beyond logical explanation. Genius he definitely was, but the nature of his genius was spelled out by his environment. Just as Mozart grew out of the musical culture of 18th century Vienna with its operas and concert halls, its abundance of teachers and intelligent audiences, Coltrane was the product of another musical culture – racist, modern America. At a certain point in history Coltrane was able to express his musical ideas with greater vision and clarity than those around him.

To give the band's sound an extra dimension Coltrane recruited multi-instrumentalist Eric Dolphy. Dolphy and Coltrane had been close friends since meeting in Los Angeles in the early 1950s. Dolphy played flute, alto saxophone and the uncommon bass clarinet. He developed a highly original sound creating an almost speech-like tone and on occasions bird-like sounds. Dolphy had previously played with Mingus and one of the founders of the avant garde movement, Ornette Coleman. Dolphy and Coltrane began to explore new playing techniques, improvisation and scale work. Already Coltrane was flirting with the sounds of the avant garde jazz movement. The potent combination of Dolphy and Coltrane was not well received by some critics who coined the repugnant term 'anti-jazz' for their music. Dolphy would leave the group in 1962, but not before making a series of live recordings with the John Coltrane Quartet at the Village Vanguard, the legendary jazz club in New York, and he was also the musical arranger for the albums *Ole* and *Africa Brass* (for contractural reasons Dolphy is named George Lane on *Ole*).

The John Coltrane Quartet was a unique partnership,

which created some of the most moving and exciting music ever recorded. It was also a band in complete harmony with itself. Tyner remembered that although Coltrane was always practising the band rehearsed no more than half a dozen times. Elvin Jones agreed: 'We never had a rehearsal, for anything. Everything that we did, all the compositions that we played – John would start by playing an outline of what we were gonna do, the new compositions for that evening. Sometimes we'd play it for a week, because we worked practically every day for years. After that time, he only had to begin an idea and all of us would immediately pick up the thread of it'.[3]

Every major jazz record label was desperate to sign Coltrane's band. In the end Impulse! struck the deal. He was given $10,000 advance against royalties rising to $20,000 in the second and third year.[4] The contract was the best deal any jazz musician had received – except for Miles Davis, of course. But it was well below the amounts given to rock and roll artists and country music stars of the time. Impulse! was the first record label to use a gatefold sleeve for just a single album. That extra space was used for photos, linear notes and personal credits. Coltrane was given complete artistic control, even over the packaging.

Coltrane and the band were not only interested in jazz. They drew artistic inspiration from a wide number of sources. They listened to Middle Eastern melodies and musical structures. From an early age Coltrane listened to classical music, in particular Debussy, Ravel and Igor Stravinsky. Coltrane believed in the universality of music and was constantly searching for a higher spiritual realisation. He told one interviewer:

> There's a lot of modal music played every day through-
> out the world. It's particularly evident in Africa – but
> if you look at Spain, Scotland, India or China, you'll
> discover this again in each case. If you want to look
> beyond the differences in style, you will con-
> firm there is a common base.[5]

The first album Coltrane recorded for Impulse!
was *Africa/Brass*. The music is very much jazz
based, but it was also heavily influenced by both
African rhythms and Indian ragas. In many ways
Africa/Brass was an unusual album to debut with
on a record label. It brought together a blend of
ten brass instruments coupled with Eric Dolphy's
reeds and flute. As Dolphy explained on the sleeve notes on
the album, 'John thought of this sound. He wanted brass,
he wanted baritone horns, he wanted that mellow sound
and power.' The second track on the album is titled 'Song of
the Underground Railroad'. As stated earlier, Coltrane had
been researching spirituals and 19th century folk songs, and
this composistion was one of the fruits of that research. 'The
Underground Railway' was the name of the escape route of
slaves fleeing from the plantations of the South. And with
other tracks on the album such as 'The Damned Don't Cry'
and 'Africa', and the ferocious energy of the bands playing,
is it any wonder that radicals and Black Nationalists began to
identify with his music?

ERIC DOLPHY

After the release of *Africa/Brass* the Coltrane Quartet made their one and only visit to Britain in November 1961. They shared the bill with the Dizzy Gillespie Quintet. British critics panned Coltrane. The review in *Melody Maker* was typical, criticising the group's hour-long set as 'belonging more to the realms of higher mathmatics than music', with the band 'all apparently playing in different tempos and frequently in different time signatures'.[6]

Ironically, over 30 years later *Melody Maker* highlighted *My Favourite Things*, one of the albums on which Coltrane's concerts were based, and descibed it as one of the most important modern jazz albums!

By now the Coltrane Quartet was progressing musically at an incredibly fast pace. The speed of that development is highlighted on the album *Live at the Village Vanguard*. It contains one tune 'Chasin' the Trane'. It is a 16-minute tenor solo covering the whole side of one album. Built up on the 12-bar blues and at over 80 choruses long, nothing like it had been heard before.

Bob Theile (the owner of Impulse!) put pressure on Coltrane and the band to make more commercial albums. He wanted Coltrane to make a *Kind of Blue* mark two. Coltrane kind of acquiesced – he brought out three albums, one entitled *Ballads*, the second with underrated crooner Johnny Hartman and the third with Duke Ellington.

Ballads is a very interesting album. By 1960 Coltrane was described by much of the musical press as the 'best of the angry tenors'. The fact is according to everyone who met him he was one of the gentlest and quietest people you could ever meet. That side of his character was on display on *Ballads*, an album of of some of the great pop ballads. When this giant of modern jazz was asked why he wanted to do the album he said 'Variety'. He meant that he wanted to introduce a change of pace. McCoy Tyner also noted that 'John is always remembered for his original material and his driving solos – but what is often forgotten is that he had the most amazing memory for all the old hits. He only had to hear them once and he could play them back to you – he really was quite amazing like that'.[7] The material Coltrane chose to play was guaranteed to please. With the exception of the track 'It's Easy to Remember', the quartet had never played any of the tunes before! The stand-out track is the Frank Sinatra classic 'Nancy (With the Laughing Face)'. It is rumoured that when Frank heard Coltrane's version he asked Count Basie, 'How about getting that cat to come and play with us some time?' Basie reportedly just laughed.

The album with Johnny Hartman is the first and last time the John Coltrane Quartet recorded with a vocalist. It is an unsatisfactory album in many ways, Coltrane's playing is well below standard and poor old Johnny Hartman doesn't even get a chance (with the exception of 'Lush Life') to sing any of the band's standards. Far more interesting is the third album – *Duke Ellington and John Coltrane*. One track stands out on the session – 'In a Sentimental Mood'. This track was written by Ellington's collaborator Billy Strayhorn, and it was always part of the Ellington band's repertoire. While the young new innovator of jazz (Coltrane) plays his solos straight it is the grand master (Ellington) who plays all the musical flourishes. Johnny Hodges, after hearing the track, said, 'As long as I've known this song, I think Coltrane gave the most beautiful interpretation I've ever heard'.[8] Hodges would have known – 'In a Sentimental Mood' had been his featured solo in the Ellington band for decades.

Impulse! may have wanted Coltrane to concentrate on making more commercial albums, but his heart wasn't in it. Despite the grillings he got from some sections of the music press, Coltrane's growing fan base and other musicians embraced the band as all-conquering heroes. Coltrane and his sidemen were constantly voted top musicians in readers' polls in 1962, 1963 and 1964.

Events elsewhere were also moving jazz music in a totally different direction. The year 1963 was another turning point for the civil rights movement. After the Montgomery bus boycott of 1955-56 King began to push through a strategy for smashing Jim Crow across all the states in the South. He believed by using mass non-violent direct action the movement could separate the hard line racists in the establishment from the owners of big business who at the end of the day would fear mass unrest because it would cut into their profits. King also believed that the violence meted out to his movement by the racists could force the national government to step in and force change.

Despite the victory in Montgomery, racists, whether they were rich businessmen, the police, members of the Klu Klux Klan or White Citizen Councils, had other plans. Robert Patterson, the leader of the White Citizen Councils, pledged, 'Mississippi would keep segregation one way or another. We will have violence and you know it'.[9]

Martin Luther King found it difficult to use the same tactics employed in Montgomery in other cities. His mass meetings and rallies left audiences spellbound, but he had failed to make a second major breakthrough. A second wave of protests began in February 1960. Four young black college students sat down in the 'whites only' section of the local Woolworths in Greensboro, North Carolina, and ordered lunch. When they were asked to leave they refused and they remained until the store closed. They returned the next day and for several days after. Within days they numbered 300 and soon the protests spread across the South.

It was young black and white college students who pioneered the fresh tactic of sit-ins in 1960 and the Freedom Rides of 1961, which inspired King to launch a new campaign. It was going to be bigger than anything seen before. The SCLC decided to stage a non-violent assault on Birmingham, Alabama. Birmingham was the symbolic bastion of segregation – a city that combined the plantation attitudes of the surrounding area with the thuggery of its police commissioner, Eugene T 'Bull' Connor. Everyone knew the fight was going to be hard. King told the congregation of a Birmingham church, 'Some of the people sitting here today will not come back alive from this campaign'.[10] King was right.

On 2 May 1963 the battle for Birmingham began. Taylor Branch, in his magnificent account of the life of Martin Luther King describes the start of the campaign:

When the doors of the 16th Street Baptist Church opened...a line of 50 teenagers emerged two abreast, singing. The waiting police detail hauled them into jail wagons, as usual, and only the youth of the demonstrators distinguished the day until a second line emerged, then a third and many more. Children as young as six years old held their ground until their arrest. Amid mounting confusion police commanders called in school buses for jail transport and sent reinforcements to intercept stray lines that slipped past them toward the downtown business district. Not a few of the onlookers in Kelly Ingram Park were dismayed to see their own disobedient offspring in the line, and the conflicting emotions of centuries played on their faces until some finally gave way. One elderly woman ran alongside the arrest line shouting, 'Sing, children, sing!'[11]

Within days 2,500 protesters swamped Birmingham's jails. When the protest flagged, King and the other Birmingham leaders went to jail. When Bull Connor set the police dogs onto the demonstrators King told one church congregation, 'When I was young I was dog-bitten for nothing. So I don't mind being bitten by a dog for standing up for freedom'.[12]

The protests had a massive impact. US government statistics record that there were 758 demonstrations against racism and 14,753 arrests in 186 US cities in the ten weeks that followed Birmingham.[13] The protests at Birmingham and elsewhere culminated in the 200,000-strong march on Washington on 28 August 1963. King's 'I have a dream' speech electrified the movement. The mass protests helped pave the way for new landmark civil rights legislation.

The civil rights movement had a massive impact on white as well as black people. The magazine *Newsweek* conducted a survey which found that 80 percent of whites, including 60 percent of Southern whites, believed blacks were treated unfairly and deserved civil rights.[14] This in turn had an impact on black music. Large numbers of whites began to identify with and seek out black music. The biggest beneficiary was soul music, but a minority were drawn towards jazz.

Coltrane's music came to symbolise much of the unrest of the time. Yet Coltrane on several occasions himself protested that was not the case, and that his playing was not an overt statement of political anger – he even said, 'If it is interpreted as anger, it is taken the wrong way'.[15] Yet Coltrane's statements are in direct contradiction to his actions. He wrote two songs in support of the movement, the first 'Alabama' (see page 86) and the second 'Reverend King'. Just as importantly, he played benefits for the Student Non-Violent Coordinating Committee and for King's SCLC. Yasuhiro Fujioka has spent half of his life piecing together and recording every single track Coltrane played on and registering every single concert he played. He notes that in 1964 Coltrane played a benefit concert for SCLC in Chicago (15 February 1964), a benefit for CORE at the Five Spot in New York (19 April 1964), played a fundraiser for Freedom Ways alongside Max Roach at the Village Gate (27 December 1964) and also found time that year to organise four workshops in black community centres.[16] A similar picture can be gleaned by looking at Coltrane's benefit gigs in 1961, 1962, 1963 and 1965. Coltrane genuinely believed that he was not political – he was far more interested in spirituality. But like many great artists whether conciously or unconciously he was absorbing and interpreting the world around him. McCoy put it another way: 'John's first love was music – for him nothing else mattered. He was a humble man. He would have genuinely believed that playing a few concerts to raise funds was nothing compared to what King and the folks were doing down in Birmingham'.[17] I'll leave it up to the reader to decide how comitted Coltrane was to the civil rights movement. But as the old saying goes, actions do speak louder than words.

Shepp notes that Coltrane also conciously attempted to connect his music to the black community: 'In Chicago he always played on the South Side at McKie's – he never went to McKellys or the big joints. He'd be playing right in the [black] community. He'd always play a joint in Watts when he was in LA, and a joint in San Francisco and in New York he'd always play at the Half Note'.[18]

Coltrane was one of a whole host of jazz, rock, folk, soul singers and film stars who came out in support of the civil rights protests. Ellington composed 'King Fit the Battle of Alabam' in tribute to the Birmingham demonstrations:

Bull turned the hoses on the church people, church people,
ol' church people,
Bull turned the hoses on the church people and the water
came splashing, dashing, crashing.
Freedom rider, ride, Freedom rider, go to town.
Y'all and us gonna git on the bus,
Y'all aboard, sit down, sit tight, sit down!

Ellington hailed the victory at Birmingham as 'a beautiful bright light of hope'.[19] Others were less impressed. Malcolm X described the march on Washington as a 'one-day integrated picnic'. Malcolm publicly criticised King's strategy of non-violence as 'this little passive resistance or wait-until-you-change-your-mind-and-then-let-me-up philosophy'.[20]

However, in 1964 Malcolm would break from the Nation of Islam, stating, 'The messenger [Elijah Muhammad] should have done more. People in the civil rights movement have been brutalised, and we haven't done anything to help them'.[21] Malcolm's growing frustrations with the Nation of Islam reflected the growing bitterness of blacks in the Northern ghettos – a bitterness that was going to explode in every major city in America.

Funeral of the four murdered girls, Birmingham, Alabama, 1963 (see page 86).
Photograph by Danny Lyon

John Coltrane
'Alabama' Live at Birdland (Impulse!)

On the Sunday morning of 15 September 1963 a dozen sticks of dynamite were planted in the basement of the 16th Street Baptist Church in Birmingham, Alabama. At 10.25am the bomb went off, killing four young black girls aged between 11 and 14. The bombing was organised by white racists who were protected by the authorities in an attempt to terrorise the civil rights protests that were sweeping the area.

Coltrane wrote the song 'Alabama' in response to the Birmingham church bombing. He patterned his saxophone lines on the cadence of Martin Luther King's funeral speech. Midway through the song, mirroring the point in the sermon where King transforms his mourning into a statement of renewed determination for the struggle against racism, Elvin Jones's drumming rises from a whisper to a pounding rage. He wanted this crescendo to signify the rising of the civil rights movement.

'Alabama', along with Bob Dylan's 'Blowing in the Wind' and Sam Cooke's 'A Change is Gonna Come', perfectly expresses the mood and emotions of that time.

07 / Rise of the avant garde

The John Coltrane Quartet reached its musical peak when it recorded the album *A Love Supreme* in 1964. It is a musical tour de force. *A Love Supreme* is Coltrane's most profoundly spiritual statement and captures the essence of gospel music through jazz. Coltrane's concern for humanity came from his deep-seated spirituality and religious convictions. He didn't follow an organised religion – his faith was a mixture of Christianity, Budhism, Hinduism and a belief in cosmology.

Like most black gospel music, *A Love Supreme* can be interpreted in two ways. Firstly, it can be understood as a eulogy to god and an affirmation in the belief in a higher being. There is no doubt Coltrane saw the album length suite as his gift to god. Today almost every hip hop and soul album has the obligatory dedication to the Almighty.

When Coltrane dedicated *A Love Supreme* to god he was probably the first major jazz musician to make such an open declaration.

But gospel music can be, and has been used as, a rallying cry against oppression on earth. Martin Luther King often used religious parables and stories as a way of giving his supporters confidence in the battles they faced. *A Love Supreme* straddles both stools. According to Archie Shepp the timing of the album's release matched a palpable step-up in the assertive nature of black protest. 'When *A Love Supreme* was released people weren't singing "Mercy, Mercy" any more. Then people were marching in Selma. Then Malcolm was preaching in the temple'.[1]

The four-note bass motif that starts *A Love Supreme* and which is restated throughout the piece is probably the best known in the whole of modern jazz. Rather than try and describe this amazing work to the reader, it makes far more sense to dust down your old copy or go and buy one and listen to it yourself. It really is one of the most important albums of the 20th century. The album sold around 500,000 copies in the first year of its release.

Great jazz albums are usually made by groups who have attained a measure of mutual understanding. Very great albums are almost always made by groups on the brink of splitting up. By the autumn of 1964 the quartet had reached that point. Coltrane was already looking for a new musical direction.

He didn't have to look far. Ornette Coleman released the album *Free Jazz* in 1960. It ushered in a new school of jazz known as 'new jazz', 'free jazz' or 'the avant garde'.

The sound Coleman created was unlike anything recorded before. He assembled together an amazing line up of eight musicians – Coleman (saxes), Don Cherry (pocket trumpet), Freddie Hubbard (trumpet), Eric Dolphy (bass clarinet), Charlie Haden (bass), Scot LaFaro (bass) and Ed Blackwell and Billy Higgins on drums. The music was one continuous free improvisation with only a few brief preset sections. Both rhythm sections play in relative time, allowing the horn sections to create a completely free sound over the top. None of the musicians knew how long it would last – in fact, it lasted for 38 minutes, the length of an album. I think it is possible to describe the music like an abstract painting with flashes of music replacing swathes of colour. The Jackson Pollock album cover was not an accident – it fitted the music perfectly.

When the Coleman band was appearing at the Five Spot in New York in 1960, John Coltrane was frequently in the audience. Charlie Haden, Coleman's bassist, recounts: 'Coltrane was in the club every night, hanging out; he would usually sit at the same table and listen to every note we played... He was very, very serious, and determined to put what he learned from Ornette into his own music.' Later that year Coltrane recorded with the other three quarters of Coleman's quartet – trumpeter Don Cherry, bassist Charlie Haden and drummer Ed Blackwell. The result was the album *The Avant Garde*. Sadly it fell victim to Atlantic Records' policy of bringing out records very slowly and did not see the light of day until 1966. By that time free jazz had evolved much further and therefore the album was not the pathbreaker it could have been.

Many critics hated Ornette's album *Free Jazz*, describing it as an unintelligible cacophony. According to Ornette's friend and jazz musician Dewey Redman several key jazz musicians – Dexter Gordon, Sonny Stitt and even Miles Davis – snubbed the young musical radicals and the music they were making. This should be no surprise. Most major advances in art, jazz included, are derided when they first come out. Anything new and original is often shocking – precisely because it challenges old concepts and creates a new path for others to follow. Of course not all avant garde art or music is good, but it is amazing how many art movements and music developments labelled avant garde become in later years mainstream, as a wider number of people begin to understand and appreciate the artists' intentions.

A whole host of jazz musicians and groups were being drawn into free jazz. They included Sun Ra, Archie Shepp, Albert Ayler and Pharaoh Sanders. They became fascinated by the music because it gave them almost complete freedom of expression. It was also a technically complex music. They began playing music with polyrhythms – beats that shift in and out of conventional musical time. It was a musical style which had much more in common with African rhythms than it did with Western music.

Coltrane was drawn towards this new musical school. From 1961 he was experimenting with free jazz. But at first he was very nervous about making such a radical musical departure. He told the British music paper *Melody Maker*, 'Whenever I make a change, I'm a little worried that it may puzzle people. And sometimes I deliberately delay things for this reason. But after a while I find there is nothing else I can do but go ahead.'

When Coltrane released the album *Ascension* in the summer of 1965, he threw his lot in with the free jazz movement. What makes this transformation remarkable is the fact that despite having just released *A Love Supreme*, one of the most successful jazz albums of all time, Coltrane was prepared to make such a huge musical break. No other major jazz figure made the switch to 'free jazz'.

Just like Coleman's band five years earlier, Coltrane only sketched out the roughest of musical plans for *Ascension*. He drafted in new musicians to play with the standard quartet – they included Freddie Hubbard and Dewey Johnson (trumpet), Marion Brown and John Tchicai (alto saxophone), Pharoah Sanders and Archie Shepp (tenor saxophone) and Art Davis (bass). The music was pure improvisation. Unlike Ornette Coleman on *Free Jazz*, Coltrane also freed up the bass players and Elvin on drums – so that they were also playing totally free. This album represents another major jazz milestone on a scale that is just as impressive as *A Love Supreme*.

Coltrane was taking the music to new heights. He was now playing two hour long solos on stage, while percussionists, harpists and various other instruments were added to the sound. Coltrane very rapidly moved to the forefront of the new free jazz movement.

The reception Coltrane's music received was mixed. At the *Down Beat* jazz festival in Chicago in 1965 there was a near-riot. *Down Beat* reviewer Buck Walmsley wrote:

> After the intermission the John Coltrane Quartet,
> with Archie Shepp as an added starter on tenor, gave
> as tasteless a display of musicianship as I've heard...
> Shepp and Coltrane seemed to be more interested
> in trying to out-honk, out-squeal and out-blast each
> other than in playing music. The one tune, 45 minute
> set was a bomb as far as most of the concert's 7,500
> attendees were concerned.[2]

Sometime earlier another critic wrote about 'a repulsive
monster, a wounded tail lashing serpent, dealing wild and
furious blows as it stiffens into a death agony'. Coltrane?
No. This quote comes from a review of Beethoven's Second
Symphony premiered in Vienna, 5 April 1803! The fact is
that many artists who push back the boundaries find their
work derided. Coltrane wasn't the first and he certainly
won't be the last.

The Chicago concert was not exceptional. Promoter
after promoter reported that large sections of the audience
would walk out in the middle of Coltrane's shows. The music
split the jazz world down the middle.

It is worth attempting to explain why Coltrane and
Shepp played the 'honks' and 'squeals' the reviewers found
so objectionable. Let's forget about jazz for a moment and
take a look at one of the most powerful soul/funk artists of
the 1960s – James Brown. Anybody fortunate to to have seen
the godfather of funk will have seen James fall to the floor, rip

off his shirt and make a whole range of passionate cries and howls. Very few critics would deny that it was an essential part of trying to convey the emotion and power of songs like 'Say it Loud, I'm Black and I'm Proud' and 'Please, Please'. Likewise the uncontrollable and at times shocking honks on Coltrane's and Shepp's horn playing were also about trying to convey raw emotion and take the music to higher levels. Far from being an aberration from the jazz tradition, which is what some people claim, these raw sounds are in fact taking the music back to its roots in the blues and field hollers.

Coltrane continued to develop the ideas he outlined on the *Ascension* album on a number of other albums recorded around the same time. *Sunship* is a brilliant if underrated work. This time the sound is stripped back to just the classic quartet – while the band creates a gentle rhythm, Coltrane sets forth with a flurry of notes.

Another album demonstrating a different musical style for Coltrane was *Kulu Se Mama*. The title track has the vocalist Juno Lewis chanting and singing a hypnotic refrain, while the rest of the band create a musical backdrop. The performance creates the feeling of a ritualistic celebration. There is one other track worth mentioning – the stunning 'Welcome' – a beautiful haunting ballad which balances the album off perfectly.

Also there is the album *Meditations*. The jazz magazine *Down Beat* used two different journalists to review the album.[3] It was like a courtroom contest between defendant and prosecutor. One reviewer gave the album five stars (top), while the other awarded it only one (bottom).[4] *Meditations* is a fascinating album. Coltrane clearly saw it as an extension of *A Love Supreme* in the sense that it was part of his consistant search in his music for a meaning to the world and to find his place within it. With the addition of Pharoah Sanders on tenor saxophone and Rashied Ali playing drums alongside Elvin it is the bridge between the end of the classic quartet and the opening of a new experimental phase in Coltrane's work.

The fact was the music was too harsh and abrasive even for the rest of the band. McCoy Tyner explained, 'I felt that if I was going to go any further musically, I would have to leave the group, and when John hired a second drummer, it became a physical necessity. I couldn't hear myself'.[5] Elvin Jones was just as angry – the inclusion of Rashied Ali made him feel redundant. At a concert the band played at Stanford University, Jones carefuly placed his drum sticks atop of his bass drum at the conclusion of a Coltrane solo and waited out the rest of the number in the wings rather than play a drum solo with Ali. One by one the band quit. By the end of 1965 the quartet was history.

Coltrane moved quickly. He opened up his group and surrounded himself with young musicians. Also his wife Alice Coltrane (piano), Pharaoh Sanders (saxophone) and Rashied Ali (drums) became a more fixed part of his band.

Alice McLeod (Coltrane) was born in Detroit in 1937. Alice studied classical music before moving to Paris in 1959 to play alongside the great Bud Powell. She returned to the US and played with a number of experimental jazz groups. She ended up meeting Coltrane, when the band she was in supported the Coltrane Quartet when they played in Detroit in 1963. She started to play alongside Coltrane by the end of 1965. To this day Pharoah Sanders continues to be a disciple of Coltrane's. Born in Little Rock, Arkansas in 1940 he started out his musical career playing in R&B groups. Sanders moved to New York in 1960 and ended up playing with Sun Ra. Things moved on very quickly for him recording as a band leader for both Impulse! and ESP. Rashied Ali was born Robert Patterson in 1935 in Philadelphia. He moved to New York in 1963 and worked with Sun Ra, Archie Shepp and Pharoah Sanders.

Coltrane hung out and played with the cream of the avant garde movement. Not only did he influence them (half the artists who signed to Impulse! were recommended by Coltrane), they drove him forward to become even more musically adventurous.

It was during this time that Coltrane complained of stomach pains and was forced to cancel a number of concerts. Time was running out for Coltrane. Just like the early bebop stars playing in the big bands, he was trying to cram as many musical ideas into his music as he possibly could. Unlike most musicians Coltrane used the recording studio as a place to experiment and create new soundscapes. One of the final albums Coltrane recorded was *Interstellar Space*. The six relatively short songs are a dual between Coltrane and Ali. This is a remarkable album. Coltrane starts at an incredible pace and ends at an incredible pace and there is no let up in between. Ali's drumming style is even freer than Elvin's. In the sleeve notes he describes what he was trying to do: 'If you listen to *Interstellar Space*, you can hear that some things are going on that's holding the whole thing together. I'm not playing regular time, but the feeling of regular time is there. I'm thinking in time. We'd start out in three or four; five-eight or six-eight, whatever. I would anchor it in my mind, but play everything not on it, but against it.' *Interstellar Space* was released in 1974, seven years after Coltrane's death. However of all the posthumous releases, and there have been many, it has had the biggest impact on a new generation of saxophone players.

Impulse! have only just, at the time of writing, released one more gem – *John Coltrane, The Olatunji Concert: The Last Live Recording*. It captures perfectly the raw intense energy and rage of the Coltrane band in the last few months. The concert was a fundraiser. Olatunji was trying to raise funding for a school to teach African history, culture and music. The poster advertising the concerts shows the outline of a map of Africa with a picture of Coltrane in the middle. Listening to the music, it is hard not to believe that it reflected the growing turmoil and protest movements that were sweeping America in the late 1960s. In fact Coltrane's new young drummer Rashied Ali said as much:

> Those were trying times in the 1960s. We had the civil rights thing going on, we had King, we had Malcolm, we had the Panthers. There was so much diversity happening. People were screaming for their rights and wanting to be equal, be free. And naturally, the music reflects that whole period...that whole time definitely influenced the way we played. I think that's

where really free form came into it. Everybody wanted to get away from the rigid thing, away from what was happening before; they wanted to relate to what was happening now, and I'm sure that the music came out of the whole thing.[6]

During the autumn of 1964 a series of avant garde jazz concerts took place in New York. It was no coincidence that the title chosen for the series was 'The October Revolution'. This was a clear reference to the 1917 Russian Revolution.[7] Interestingly free jazz became popular in France and Eastern Europe at the time. The explanation for this is obvious. France in 1968 had gone through a radical upheaval, first with a massive wave of student marches and occupations, followed by a general strike involving millions of workers. The movement nearly brought the state crashing down. The 'revolutionary' energy of the music fitted the times perfectly. Just as Paris had been a Mecca for many black jazz musicians of the bebop era – Bud Powell, Kenny Clarke and Hal Singer – the city once again attracted a new generation of free jazz muscians including the likes of Archie Shepp, Oliver Lake and a host of musicians from the Association for the Advancement of Creative Musicians. Eastern European musicians were also attracted to free jazz because it was music without rules – it acted as a metaphor for their hopes and aspirations and their desire to be free. Also because the authorities tolerated free jazz it was possible to play this subversive music with the acceptence of the state and at the same time cock a snook at the authorities. And finally for a few musicians it was a passport out of the East to play and perform in Europe and US.

As a sign of how political things had become, bebop hero Dizzy Gillespie even ran for president in 1964. In one way Gillespie was mocking the system, but there was also a serious point to his campaign. The presidential election was a three-way contest that included segregationist Alabama governor George Wallace, war-hawk senator Barry Goldwater and Lyndon Johnson – Gillespie wanted to see an alternative. Gillespie's platform included changing the name White House to Blues House, disbanding the FBI and forcing job applicants to wear sheets so potential employers couldn't tell their race. He named Miles Davis his future head of the CIA, Max Roach his minister of defence and Charles Mingus his minister of peace.[8]

While the fight for civil rights was confined to the Southern states, it remained under the control of King. When the movement spread to the Northern ghettos it exploded. Northern blacks already had civil rights. Yet they faced massive economic discrimination. By 1960, 70 percent of all employed black people were in unskilled and semi-skilled blue collar or service jobs. On average whites were paid almost twice as much as blacks, and unemployment rates for blacks remained more than twice those for whites.[9] In Philadelphia, the city in which Coltrane grew up, unemployment among black youth had reached 70 percent by 1964.[10] In Boston in 1963 CORE reported that 27 percent less was spent per pupil in black than in white schools.[11]

Although blacks had won their civil rights, real equality

seemed as distant as ever. It became commonplace among urban blacks to ask what use was the right to eat in an integrated restaurant if you couldn't afford the price of a hamburger. Malcolm X, who so eloquently expressed the feelings and aspirations of the poor and working class blacks in Northern cities said a few years earlier:

> We don't want leaders who are hand picked by white men. We don't want any more Uncle Toms. We don't want any more leaders who are puppets and parrots for the white man.[12]

As the fight against racism and discrimination moved to the Northern cities of America the protests took a different and more radical turn. American cities went up in flames. These were not riots – they were urban uprisings. There were nine such uprisings in 1965, 38 in 1967 and 131 in the first six months of 1968. A report of the Detroit uprising in *Time* magazine gives a flavour of the scale of the protests:

> In the violent summer of 1967, Detroit became the scene of the bloodiest uprisings in a half century and the costliest in terms of property damage in US history. At the week's end, there were 41 known dead, 347 injured, 3,800 arrested. Some 5,000 people were homeless...while 1,300 buildings had been reduced to mounds of ashes and bricks, and 2,700 businesses sacked. Damage estimates reached $500 million.[13]

The old leaders of the civil rights movement were left floundering. Their calls for passive non-violence fell on deaf ears. While King and the leaders of the SCLC were talking about non-violent action, blacks in the inner city were rioting. The following is an account of a meeting addressed by Martin Luther King just after the uprising had ended in Watts in 1965:

> King spoke to an overflow crowd…he was heckled, jeered and rejected. The Northern ghetto Negro was showing a readiness to fight for more than the right to vote. 'All over America,' Dr King said, 'the Negro must join hands –'
>
> 'And burn,' interrupted a man standing on the edge of a crowd.
>
> A woman told Dr King, 'Let Chief Parker and Mayor Yorty come down here and see how we live.'
>
> Dr King promised to try and get Chief Parker and Mayor Yorty down to Watts. 'I know you'll be courteous to them,' he said.
>
> The crowd roared with laughter… The Watts rebels were looking for a new leader.[14]

King was even more shocked when later that day he came across a young man who proudly told him: 'We won, we won.' Looking at the mayhem and destruction King asked how he could say that. 'Because we made them pay attention to us,' was his response. It was not an isolated sentiment. A survey conducted in Watts found that 58 percent of the residents thought that the effect of the riot would be favourable, and only 18 percent that it would be unfavourable. One respondent commented:

> Things will be better. We will have new buildings, and the whites now realise that the Negro isn't going to be pushed around like before.[15]

Non-violent resistance was replaced by militant action. A new phrase was coined – 'Black Power' – and a new generation of activists led and gave expression to this movement. Miles Davis was clear that this militancy and anger were reflected in the music of Coltrane. He wrote:

> He [Coltrane] was expressing through music what H Rap Brown and Stokely Carmichael and the Black Panthers and Huey Newton were saying with their words, what the Last Poets and Amiri Baraka were saying in poetry.
> He was their torch bearer in jazz, now ahead of me. He played what they felt inside and were expressing through riots – 'burn baby burn' – that were taking place everywhere... It was all about revolution for a lot of young black people – Afro hairdos, dashikis, Black Power, fists raised in the air. Coltrane was their symbol, their pride – their beautiful black revolutionary pride.[16]

It would be hard to imagine any artist working or living in the Northern ghettos failing to absorb the turmoil going on around them – and it is worth remembering that Coltrane and the free jazz musicians consciously related to the ghettos, just like today's rap artists do. Coltrane never used his music as a political tool in the same way as artists like Max Roach or in later years Archie Shepp did. But there can be no doubt about the impact and emotions stirred by the music that he created. Mike Canterino, the owner of the Half Note club in New York, described what it was like when Coltrane's band played:

> The audiences at the Half Note were mixed. We seemed to attract the most politically advanced blacks whenever Trane [Coltrane] was appearing. He'd take a long solo, probably close to an hour and these guys would be shouting, 'Freedom now!'[17]

It is worth answering the critics who say that Coltrane was not interested in this reaction to his music. Elvin Jones, who had by this time left the band, claimed, 'If he didn't like the response he would have changed style. John understood the world around him – privately, I think he loved it.'

Not every avant garde jazz musician was a revolutionary, but for many the aesthetic revolution was closely connected with the political one. For example, the saxophone player Archie Shepp described himself as 'an anti-fascist artist'. At a panel discussion on jazz, Shepp went even further, stating:

> [Jazz is] one of the most meaningful social, aesthetic contributions to America. It is anti-war, it is opposed to the US war in Vietnam, it is for Cuba, it is for the

liberation of all people... Why is that so? Because jazz is a music born out of oppression, born out of the enslavement of my people.[18]

Charlie Haden released *Liberation Music Orchestra* in 1969. The album contained four Spanish Civil War songs, a number inspired by the riot outside the Chicago Democratic convention, a commemoration to Cuban revolutionary Che Guevara and a version of the civil rights hymn 'We Shall Overcome'.

The Black Power movement scared the authorities. Musicians like Miles Davis and Archie Shepp who came out in support of the struggle or criticised the music establishment were labelled by some sections of the music press as 'reverse racists'.[19] This was absurd – Davis regularly hired white musicians. When he took flack for hiring white saxophone player Lee Konitz, he countered his critics by saying:

I just told them if a guy could play as good as Lee played I would hire him every time and I wouldn't give a damn if he was green with red breath. I'm hiring a motherfucker to play, not for what colour he is.[20]

The fight against racism gave inspiration to the rise of the women's movement and the fight for gay liberation. But the largest of all the struggles was the anti Vietnam War movement. In April 1965 400,000 marched in New York. In November of the same year 100,000 demonstrated in Washington and 30,000 activists surrounded the Pentagon, which was guarded by armed troops.[21] Thousands refused to fight in the Vietnam War. Reggie Workman, a bassist in Coltrane's band, was called up to join the army to fight in Vietnam. He told them bluntly that he didn't believe in the policy of the country and that he wasn't going to 'put his life on the line when there was a fight right here in this country with which he should be involved'.[22]

Coltrane and Tyner also came out against the Vietnam War. When asked to comment on it in 1966 Coltrane said, 'Well, I dislike war – period. So therefore, as far as I'm concerned it should stop; it should have already stopped. And any other war. Now as far as those issues behind it, I don't understand them well enough to tell you how this should be brought about. I only know it should be stopped'.[23]

Despite all the hostile press, Coltrane continued to be an international jazz superstar. In 1966 Coltrane's new band toured Japan. When they arrived in Japan a crowd several thousand strong surrounded the plane. As the band was walking down the ramp, bassist Jimmy Garrison nudged Coltrane and said, 'You know of any bigshot on the plane?' Coltrane shrugged his shoulders and then spotted banners that read 'Welcome John Coltrane'.[24]

During the tour Coltrane visited the War Memorial Park in Nagasaki where he asked for 'peace on earth'. He spoke out against injustice. He told one interviewer, 'I believe with brotherhood there would be no poverty. And also there would be no war'.[25] These were the values and themes that he developed in his music.

08 / Jazz after Coltrane

On the morning of Sunday 16 July 1967 John Coltrane was rushed to hospital suffering from stomach pains – he was diagnosed with cancer of the liver. He died the next day, two months before what would have been his 41st birthday. At his funeral his poem 'A Love Supreme' was read out, and the quartets of Albert Ayler and Ornette Coleman both played. Ayler recalls that during his performance he stopped twice and screamed, not with his saxophone but with his voice, the first scream a cry of pain and the other a shout of joy that Coltrane's music would live on.[1]

But within two years of Coltrane's death the 'free jazz' movement collapsed. Why? Clearly the sudden and tragic deaths of Coltrane and Albert Ayler, two years later, deprived the movement of its two main driving forces. This was a blow from which the scene did not and could not recover. The assassinations of Martin Luther King and Malcolm X had a similar impact on the fight against racism in the US. Also as the Black Power movement fell apart, through a mixture of state repression and internal divisions, was it any wonder that a music that was so closely connected to the movement should collapse with it?

Also I think some parallels can be drawn with abstract visual art. I would argue that those artists who strip down their work to the point where they paint a blank canvas white or just a block of colour have taken that art form to its furthest point of abstraction. Coltrane produced the musical equivalent of the white canvas with *Ascension* and so too did Albert Ayler with his album *Spiritual Unity*. You can only take this parallel so far – free jazz has a much greater relationship with its audience and is very much music of the moment. In many ways Coltrane, Ayler and Coleman took free jazz as far as it could go, but the important thing to remember is that Coltrane and the others did create a new canvas, new structures from which others could set off on a new course and one on which the musicians who followed could add their own unique sounds.

Also by the time of Coltrane's death 'free jazz' had found itself in a musical cul de sac. Just like swing, bebop and hard bop, 'free jazz' had run out of musical energy. Many of the founders of 'free jazz' moved on into academia.[2] Black studies and music courses provided many jazz musicians with stable jobs and took them away from playing music on a regular basis. There was also a number of musicians – Sunny Murray, Cecil Taylor and David S Ware – who throughout the 1970s, 1980s and 1990s continued to carry the torch of free jazz.

In some ways many 'free jazz' performers prided themselves on the fact that their music was not commercial. 'We're not entertainers, we're creating art' was a common refrain. I think that is a perferctly valid view to hold. In fact I would go further and say that it was, and is, essential if jazz is to develop, that more artists attempt their search for new forms of expression. The technical complexity of the music and the lack of melody meant that it was too abstract for the majority of jazz fans, let alone the bulk of music listeners. Those attending 'new jazz' concerts tended to be other jazz musicians and revolutionaries. The music failed to reach out to a mass audience – it certainly never connected with black and white youth. The Art Ensemble of Chicago, one of the most exciting avant garde bands, once found themselves playing to just three people in their hometown.[3]

Today things are different. The musical ideas that Coltrane produced that shocked the critics and left many of his fans floundering have now been incorporated into the jazz canon. Today popular jazz musicians like Joshua Redman, Courtney Pine, David Murray and Kenny Garrett often include some of the more complicated Coltrane licks into their sets. Very few people even bat an eyelid. 30 years after they were first played many of Coltrane's musical ideas have become appreciated, enjoyed and understood.

Towards the end of his life Coltrane had become increasingly worried about the musical direction he was taking. Just before his death he and his band were due to play a gig in

Detroit. They were to share the bill with Thelonious Monk and his band. Monk's band made it to the gig but Coltrane's rhythm section was snowed in. Only John and Alice Coltrane made it. Coltrane ended up playing a set with Monk. They played mostly Monk's music, in particular those tunes from their 1957 album. Afterwards the promoter told Coltrane, 'I'm rather glad your rhythm section didn't make it tonight.' 'I thought you'd feel that way,' Coltrane replied. 'You know, I often wonder if what I'm doing now is the right way to play'.[4]

The second blow was struck even before 'new jazz' had developed. It was the emergence of rock and roll, and rhythm and blues (or, as it is better known today, soul music). Rock and soul pushed jazz to the perimeters of the music world. According to chart magazine *Billboard International*, by 1972 only 1.3 percent of all records sold in the US were jazz, which compared to over 75 percent of sales attributed to rock and soul artists.[5] Not many young kids were humming along to John Coltrane – they were dancing in the streets to the sound of Motown and the Beatles. Rock, funk and soul music were angry and rebellious. They expressed in a much more direct and dynamic way the spirit of the times. During the 1930s and 1950s, when jazz music was at its most popular, musicians who wanted to make statements about the world they lived in were by and large forced to codify their messages. Twenty five years later James Brown could openly sing 'Say it Loud – I'm Black and I'm Proud' and Aretha Franklin could demand 'Respect', and it didn't harm their musical careers.

The growing popularity of soul and rock forced jazz to

adapt. During the late 1960s Davis, along with a number of jazz musicians, became influenced by funk music. Davis's music combined jazz with the funk of James Brown, the soul of Sly Stone and the rock of Jimi Hendrix. The result was *Bitches Brew*, an album that changed the face of jazz. It ushered in jazz-rock and jazz-fusion, a style of jazz that would dominate during the 1970s.

Jazz is more popular today than it has been for several decades, and it is now firmly part of the establishment. Wynton Marsalis's Lincoln Centre Jazz Orchestra is promoted by the US government around the world. Jazz is now studied at most major US universities. It remains an important influence on a diverse range of music – Latin jazz, rap and rock.

Today you can hear the influence of free jazz in the work of hip hop artists like DJ Shadow, Anti Pop Consortium and Q Tip and and a host of drum and bass musicians including Afronaught, Roni Size and DJ Spooky.

Miles Davis wrote in his autobiography that jazz was becoming 'the music of the museum'.[6] It is true that many jazz musicians seem content with trying to master the techniques of their musical heroes, instead of setting the musical pace. This is not the first time that jazz has suffered from artistic stagnation. In the late 1920s and once again in the early 1950s jazz declined both in popularity and as a musical force. However, it is possible for a music form to revive. For example, country music was dead in the water 20 years ago. But in recent years a new generation of musicians has gone back to the music's roots and redefined the sound. However, it is important to remember that there are thousands of jazz musicians all around the world creating exciting and innovative music.

The argument that jazz is in decline also partially explains why Coltrane's music is experiencing such a renaissance. Musically he represents the high point of jazz in the second half of the 20th century. Almost every single Coltrane album has now been reissued. The so called 'Classic Quartet' albums are universally regarded as some of the greatest jazz recordings ever. Coltrane's influence shines through almost every modern day saxophone player. Like so much art initially labelled avant garde, Coltrane's music has gone from the fringes of cultural expression into its mainstream.

As we enter the 21st century, where is jazz going? I think it's too early to say. But in the immortal words of Charlie Parker, 'You can never tell what you'll be thinking tomorrow. But I can definitely say that jazz won't stop. It will continue to go forward'.[7]

Notes

Introduction

1   Frank Kofsky, *Black Nationalism and the Revolution in Music* (Pathfinder, 1970), p65.

2   Craig Werner, *A Change is Gonna Come* (Plume, 1998), p125.

3   Leon Trotsky, *Literature and Revolution* (Redwords, 1991), p207.

4   LeRoi Jones, *Blues People* (Payback Press, 1995), p137. When Jones wrote his book in 1963 the term Negro was a progressive term used by blacks and anti-racists. Throughout this book I have maintained the use of the original language even though it may jar to a modern reader.

5   Notes from the Duke Ellington album *The Blanton Webster Band* (BlueBird, 1940-42).

6   Interview with McCoy Tyner, *Socialist Review* 245 (October 2000).

7   Geoffrey C Ward and Ken Burns, *Jazz: A History of America's Music* (Pimlico, 2001), p188.

The early years

1   Eric Hobsbawm, *The Jazz Scene* (Weidenfeld, 1989), p44.

2   Interview with Dizzy Gillespie on BBC Radio for part of the *The History of Jazz*.

3   Interview with John Coltrane in *Jazz Review* (January 1959).

4   Ashley Kahn, *A Love Supreme: The creation of John Coltrane's classic album*, (Granta 2002), p7

5   Eric Hobsbawm, *The Jazz Scene*, op cit, p64.

6   LeRoi Jones, op cit, p159.

7   Eric Hobsbawm, *The Jazz Scene*, op cit, p53.

8   Scott DeVeaux, *Bebop: A Social and Musical History* (Picador, 1999), p88.

9   As above, p258.

10   Ashley Kahn, op cit, p7.

11   Eric Hobsbawm, *Uncommon People: Resistance, Rebellion and Jazz* (Weidenfeld and Nicolson, 1988), p277.

12   As above, p277.

13   Interview with John Coltrane in *Jazz Review* (January 1957).

14   J C Thomas, *Coltrane: Chasin' the Trane* (Da Capo, 1975), p14.

15   For a detailed account of the CPUSA's fight to organise among blacks, Mark Naison, *Communists in Harlem During the Depression* (Grove Press, 1983), cannot be beaten.

16   Abel Meeropol wrote under the pen name Lewis Allan and was a secret member of the CPUSA.

17   *Guardian*, 16 February 2001.

18   Michael Denning, *The Cultural Front* (Verso, 1996), p309.

19   As above, p316.

20   Geoffrey C Ward and Ken Burns, op cit, p240.

Bebop

1   Gene Santoro, *Myself When I Am Real: The Life and Music of Charles Mingus* (Oxford 2000), p55.

2   LeRoi Jones, op cit, p177.

3   Lewis Porter, *John Coltrane: His Life and Music* (University of Michigan Press, 1999), p39.

4   C O Simpkins, *Coltrane: A Biography* (Black Classic Press, 1989), p40.

5   Scott DeVeaux, op cit, p237.

6   Nelson George, *The Death of Rhythm and Blues* (Omnibus, 1989), p23.

7   Ross Russell, *Bird Lives!* (Quartet Books, 1973), p78.

8   Gene Santoro, op cit, p97.

9   Black swing band leaders Fletcher Henderson, Benny Carter, Duke Ellington, Coleman Hawkins and Don Redman all went to college – a career avenue only open to the black middle class.

10   LeRoi Jones, op cit, p188.

11   Malcolm X, with the assistance of Alex Haley, *The Autobiography of Malcolm X* (Penguin, 1983), p135.

12   Ross Russell, op cit, p74.

13   Interview with John Coltrane in *Down Beat* (29 September 1960).

14   'Trane on Track', *Down Beat* (12 April 1958).

15   Interview with McCoy Tyner. August 2000.

16   Scott DeVeaux, op cit, p249.

17   Ross Russell, op cit, pp159-160.

18   Michael Denning, op cit, p336.

19   As above, p335.

Cool

1   Frank Kofsky, *John Coltrane and the Jazz Revolution of the 1960s* (Pathfinder, 1998), p43.

2   Lewis Porter, op cit, p85.

3   J C Thomas, op cit, p66.

4   Michael Ryan and Douglas Kellner, *Camera Politica: The Politics and Ideology of Contemporary Hollywood film* (Indiana University Press, 1990), p2.

5   Ethlie Ann Vare, *Frank Sinatra and the American Dream* (Boulevard Books, 1995), p65.

6   Mike Marqusee, *Redemption Song: Muhammad Ali and the Spirit of the Sixties* (Verso, 1999), p36.

Hard bop

1   Miles Davis with Quincy Troupe, *Miles: The Autobiography* (Picador, 1989), p186.

2   As above, p202.

3   Ashley Kahn, op cit, page 24

4   Coltrane on Coltrane, *Down Beat* September 1960.

5   Frank Kofsky, *John Coltrane and the Jazz revolution of the 1960s*, op cit, pp74-75.

6   Interview with Art Blakey in *Down Beat* (September 1960).

7   Mike Marqusee, op cit, p54.

8   Sleeve notes by Benny Green for *Kind of Blue* (Columbia, 1959).

9   As above.

10   Interview with John Coltrane in *Down Beat*, (September 1960)

11   Interview with the author, August 2002.

12   For a more detailed analysis of Coltrane's 'sheets of sound' technique, see Valerie Wilmer, *As Serious as Your Life: The Story of the New Jazz* (Quartet Books, 1977).

Standing out against the stream

1   Gene Santoro, op cit, p198.

2   Sleeve notes for Sonny Rollins, *Freedom Now* (Riverside 1958).

3   Gene Santoro, op cit, pp222-223.

4   As above, p328.

5   Michael Denning, op cit, p336.

6   Val Wilmer, op cit, page 23.

The Classic Quartet

1   Interview in *Register* 1960.

2   Interview with the author, October 2000.

3   Interview with the author, August 2002.

4   Lewis Porter, op cit, p190.

5   As above, p211.

6   *Melody Maker*, 18 November 1961.

7   McCoy Tyner, interview with the author, August 2000.

8   J C Thomas, op cit, p155.

9   Jack M Bloom, *Class, Race and the Civil Rights Movement* (Indiana University Press, 1987) p98.

10   Taylor Branch, *Pillar of Fire: America in the King Years 1963- 1965* (Simon and Schuster, 1998), p26.

11   As above, p77.

12   As above, p76.

13   As above, p84.

14   Interview with Ira Gitler in Alyn Shipton, *A New History of Jazz*, (Continuum 2001).

15   Yasuhiro Fujioka, *John Coltrane: a Discography and Musical Biography* (The Scarecrow Press, 1995), p242.

16   Interview with the author, August 2000.

17   Ashley Kahn, op cit, p68.

18   Taylor Branch, op cit, p136.

19   As above, p517.

20   L Perry, *Malcolm: A Life* (New York, 1991), p213.

21   Taylor Branch, op cit, p14.

Rise of the avant garde

1   Ashley Kahn, op cit, p160.

2   J C Thomas, op cit, p198.

3   *Meditations* was recorded in the autumn of 1965.

4   J C Thomas, op cit, p217.

5   Len Lyons, *The Great Jazz Pianists* (Da Capo, 1983), p239.

6   Alyn Shipton, op cit, p798.

7   Frank Kofsky, op cit, p139.

8   Gene Santoro, op cit, p228.

9   Peter Alexander, *Racism, Resistance and Revolution* (Bookmarks, 1987) p75.

10   Bureau of the Census, 1964.

11   Jack M Bloom, op cit, p 190.

12   Recording of Malcolm X speaking in New York, probably 1964,

on First Amendment Records bootleg.

13   *Time* magazine, 4 August, 1967.

14   Della Rossa, *The Black Uprisings* (Merit 1966), p11.

15   Martin Luther King, *Where Do We Go From Here: Chaos or Community* (Harper and Row, 1967), p112.

16   Miles Davis with Quincy Troupe, op cit, p275.

17   J C Thomas, op cit, p169.

18   As above, p209.

19   A number of jazz musicians have argued that 'only blacks can play jazz'. This is something I reject. Of course black musicians have almost solely defined jazz music. But there have been white jazz musicians – Bill Evans, Benny Goodman and Charlie Haden – who have left a lasting mark on the music. It would also be foolish to ignore the impact white classical and rock musicians, and writers have had on jazz, let alone white audiences, managers, producers and record company owners. But of course the fact remains that, on one instrument after another, black musicians have defined the tradition.

20   Miles Davis and Quincy Troupe, op cit, p107.

21   Chris Harman, *The Fire Last Time: 1968 and After* (Bookmarks, 1988), p72.

22   C O Simkins, op cit, p141.

23   Frank Kofsky, op cit, p455.

24   J C Thomas, op cit, p209.

25   Frank Kofsky, op cit, p436.

Jazz after Coltrane

1   Valerie Wilmer, op cit, p107.

2   As above, p242.

3   Geoffrey C Ward and Ken Burns, op cit, p457.

4   J C Thomas, op cit, p206.

6   Eric Hobsbawm, *Uncommon People*, op cit, p282.

6   Miles Davis and Quincy Troupe, op cit, p381.

7   Richard Cook and Brian Morton, *The Penguin Guide to Jazz* (Penguin, 1992), p846.

John Coltrane discography

Below are some of the key albums Coltrane made (date in brackets is the year of recording, not the year of release). This is by no means complete, but it does represent most of his best work.

Coltrane (Original Jazz Classics 1957)
Blue Train (Blue Note 1957)
Giant Steps (Atlantic 1959)
Coltrane Jazz (Atlantic 1960)
The Avant-Garde (Atlantic 1960)
My Favorite Things (Atlantic 1960)
Coltrane's Sound (Atlantic 1960)
Coltrane Plays the Blues (Atlantic 1960)
Ole Coltrane (Atlantic 1961)
The Complete Africa/Brass Sessions (Impulse! 1961)
Live at the Village Vanguard (Impulse! 1961)
Coltrane (Impulse! 1962)
Ballads (Impulse! 1962)
Duke Ellington and John Coltrane (Impulse! 1962)
John Coltrane and Johnny Hartman (Impulse! 1963)
Coltrane Live at Birdland (Impulse! 1963)
Newport 1963 (Impulse! 1963)
Crescent (Impulse! 1964)
A Love Supreme (Impulse! 1964)
Ascension (Impulse! 1965)
Sun Ship (Impulse! 1965)
Meditations (Impulse! 1965)
Live at the Village Vanguard Again! (Impulse! 1966)
Interstellar Space (Impulse! 1967)
Expression (Impulse! 1967)
The Olantunji Concert: The Last Live Recordings (Impulse! 1967)

Further listening

I thought it would be worth highlighting some of the great jazz recordings of the 20th century. All of them should be available at any decent music store. Many are now available on CD. This is by no means a definitive list, and most jazz collectors will already own them. But, given the fact that 95 percent of the record buying public owns only three jazz records or less, hopefully it will be of some use!

Louis Armstrong
Hot Fives and Sevens, volumes one, two and three (JSP, 1926-29)
The founding father of modern jazz – it still sounds fresh 80 years later.

Count Basie
The Original Decca Recordings (MCA, 1937-39)
Recorded at the height of the swing era.

Ornette Coleman
The Shape of Jazz to Come (Atlantic, 1959)
Free Jazz (Atlantic, 1960)
Great albums from one of the leading lights of avant garde jazz.

Miles Davis
Cookin'/Relaxin'/Workin'/Steamin' (Prestige, 1956)
Kind of Blue (CBS, 1959)
Bitches Brew (Columbia, 1969).
The album that launched fusion/jazz rock.

Eric Dolphy
Out to Lunch (Blue Note, 1964). A great modern jazz album.

Duke Ellington
The Blanton-Webster Years (RCA Bluebird, 1940-42).
The greatest Ellington band.
Black Brown and Beige (RCA Bluebird, 1946).
At Newport (Columbia, 1956).
Recorded live at the Newport jazz festival.
New Orleans Suite (Atlantic, 1971).
A wonderful evocation of the musical traditions that go to make up jazz.

Benny Goodman

The Birth of Swing (RCA Bluebird, 1935–36).

Dexter Gordon

Our Man in Paris (Blue Note, 1963). Recorded in 1963, it was Gordon's return to his bebop past. His solo on 'Night in Tunisia' is a classic.

Charlie Haden

Liberation Music (Impulse!, 1970).

The music is inspired by the struggles in the late 1960s – included on the album are four songs from the Spanish Revolution and another dedicated to Che Guevara.

Joe Henderson

If You're Not Part of the Solution, You're Part of the Problem (Milestone, 1970).

The title of the album is taken from the writings of Black Panther Eldridge Cleaver. Recorded in the summer of 1970, it perfectly captures the anger of the declining civil rights movement. Henderson's hard bop saxophone is played with just a touch of fusion.

Andrew Hill

Point of Departure (Blue Note, 1964).

Billie Holiday

One of the great vocalists of all time – there are loads of great compilations of her work available. One to look out for is Greatest Hits Volume Two (MCA). It contains a haunting version of 'Strange Fruit', her anti-lynching song.

Wynton Marsalis

Blood on the Fields (Sony, 1997).

Marsalis's epic account of slavery in the US.

Charles Mingus

The Clown (Atlantic, 1957). Underrated album from one of jazz's great modern band leaders. Wonderful version of 'Haitian Fight Song', a celebration of the slave rebellion.

Charles Mingus Presents Charles Mingus (Candid, 1960). Contains 'Fables of Faubus'.

Oh Yeah (Atlantic, 1962).

The Black Saint and the Sinner Lady (MCA, 1963).

Also worth looking out for is the Mingus Big Band's *Blues and Politics* (Dreyfus Jazz, 1999). Many of his old band members got together and re-recorded many of Mingus's most political works.

Thelonious Monk

Genius of Modern Music volumes one and two (1947-48).
Monk/Trane (Milestone, 1973). John Coltrane with Thelonius Monk's band.

Gerry Mulligan

At Storyville (Pacific Jazz, 1956). One of the few great cool jazz recordings.

Charlie Parker

The Great Sessions 1947/48 (Jazz Anthology).
Bebop at its best. Poorly recorded but gives a flavour of the energy of the times.
The Complete Legendary Rockland Palace Concert 1952 (Jazz Classics, 1996). The only stereo recording of Parker. This is a recording of a concert in honour of Benjamin J Davis, a black Communist councillor imprisoned under the Smith act – for being a Communist.

Max Roach

Deeds not Words (OJC, 1958).
We Insist! Freedom Now Suite (Candid, 1960).
It's Time (Impulse!).
Lift Every Voice and Sing (1971).
Four classic albums chronicling the civil rights movement.

Sonny Rollins

Saxophone Colossus (OJC, 1956).
The Freedom Suite (OJC, 1958).

Archie Shepp

Four for Trane (Impulse!, 1964). Co-produced by John Coltrane
Attica Blues (Impulse!, 1972). Shepp's most political album, combining jazz and funk. One track is dedicated to George Jackson and another to the prison uprising in Attica.

Further reading

There are literally thousands of books on jazz. The books listed below are in my opinion worth checking out.

General

Eric Hobsbawm, *Uncommon People: Resistance, Rebellion and Jazz* (Weidenfeld & Nicolson, 1998)

Charlie Hore, 'Jazz: A People's Music' (article in *International Socialism* 61, Winter 1993)

LeRoi Jones, *Black Music* (Da Capo Press, 1998)

Leon Trotsky, *Literature and Revolution* (Redwords, 1991)

Geoffrey C Ward and Ken Burns, *Jazz: A History of American Music* (Pimlico, 2000)

Howard Zinn, *A People's History of the United States: From 1492 to the Present* (Longman, 1996)

Nat Shapiro and Nat Hentoff, *Hear Me Talkin to Ya* (Penguin, 1962)

The early years

Michael Denning, *The Cultural Front* (Verso, 1996)

Sidney Finkelstein, *Jazz: A People's Music* (International Publishers, 1988)

LeRoi Jones, *Blues People* (Payback Press, 1995)

Francis Newton, *The Jazz Scene* (Penguin, 1963). This book has since been republished under Eric Hobsbawm's own name (London, 1990).

Bebop

Scott DeVeaux, *BeBop: A Social and Musical History* (Picador, 1999)

Ira Gitler, *Swing to Bop* (Oxford University Press, 1986)

Ross Russell, *Bird Lives!* (Quartet Books, 1988)

The civil rights movement

Taylor Branch, *Parting the Waters: America in the King Years 1954–63* (Touchstone, 1989)

Taylor Branch, *Pillar of Fire: America in the King Years 1963–65* (Simon & Schuster, 1998)

Dan Georgakas and Marvin Surkin, *Detroit: I Do Mind Dying* (Redwords, 1998)

Chris Harman, *The Fire Last Time: 1968 and After* (Bookmarks, 1988)

Bobby Seale, Seize the Time (Hutchinson, 1970)

New jazz

Frank Kofsky, *John Coltrane and the Jazz Revolution of the 1960s* (Pathfinder, 1998)

A B Spellman, *Four Lives in the Bebop Business* (MacGibbon & Kee, 1967)

Craig Werner, *A Change is Gonna Come: Music, Race and the Soul of America* (Penguin, 1999)

Valerie Wilmer, *As Serious as Your Life* (Serpent's Tail, 1992)

Autobiographies and biographies

Miles Davis and Quincy Troupe, *Miles: The Autobiography* (Picador, 1989)

Martin Duberman, *Paul Robeson: A Biography* (New Press, 1988)

Derek Jewell, Duke: *A Portrait of Duke Ellington* (Sphere, 1978)

Mike Marqusee, *Redemption Song: Muhammad Ali and the Spirit of the Sixties* (Verso, 1999)

Lewis Porter, *John Coltrane: His Life and Music* (University of Michigan, 1998)

Gene Santoro, *Myself When I Am Real: The Life and Music of Charles Mingus* (Oxford University Press, 2000)

C O Simkins, *Coltrane: A Biography* (Black Classic Press, 1989)

J C Thomas, *Coltrane: Chasin' the Trane* (Da Capo, 1975)

Malcolm X and Alex Haley, *The Autobiography of Malcolm X* (Penguin Books, 1983)